# SPEAKING from the HEART

# SPEAKING
## from the HEART

*Richer Relationships
through Communication*

# KEN DURHAM

**SP**

## Sweet Publishing
Ft. Worth, Texas
G.R. Welch Ltd., Canada

Unless otherwise indicated, Scripture quotations are from the Holy Bible:
New International Version (NIV), copyright © 1978 by the International
Bible Society. Used by permission of Zondervan Bible Publishers.

Printed in the United States of America. All rights reserved.
10 9 8 7 6 5 4 3 2 1

Library of Congress Card Catalog Number 86-61523.

ISBN 0-8344-0136-3

This book is lovingly dedicated to my parents, Mary Lori and Ken Durham, Sr., who have always modeled for me the ways of godliness and the language of love.

# Foreword

An old Scots friend of mine has a colorful way of challenging people about any careless use of communication. "Heart your tongue!" he says in his thick burr when he overhears anyone using words to hurt or confuse others. This is his rendition of the familiar phrase, "mind your tongue!" My friend is using "heart" in the inclusive biblical sense of the mind, emotion and will. Years of experience have taught him that what's in the heart produces what's on the tongue.

In this very powerful and insightful book about communication Ken Durham shares the secret of how to "heart your communication" in relationships. Here is a book that's both biblical and practical. It sparkles with vivid illustrations of contemporary people who are discovering how to communicate from the heart. Yet this is so much more than another book on the techniques of communication. It is an impelling treatment of the deeper causes of our inabilities to communicate in depth. That analysis is perfectly balanced with a stunning description of how God can give us a new heart filled with his Spirit so that we can communicate creatively, rather than negatively.

We all experience the excruciating pain of being misunderstood. Often it's not just by those we consider less than friends —it's the people we love. We try hard to say what we mean, and yet it's amazing sometimes what people hear. Communication has been defined as the "ground of meeting," but frequently in our conversations we miss rather than meet. Misunderstandings, broken relationships and hurting memories over what has been said to us or by us fill our lives with stress. So, communication is still one of our greatest problems.

Doing something about it is also one of our most crucial responsibilities. Eventually we have to come to the place where, instead of stewing over our lack of communication, we seek the Lord's help in becoming persons who communicate in the most loving, caring, healing and effective way.

In this book, Ken Durham helps us admit our need to become more powerful communicators. He shows us how to discover the power source for maximum communication. Then he gives us a picture of the dynamic communicators we can become. And, it all begins with the heart. We can be part of a new breed of adventurers in the Spirit who speak from the heart.

You are in for an exciting time reading this book. You'll not be the same when you're finished.


**Lloyd John Ogilvie**

# Contents

# 1

# *Created to Communicate*

"**W**hat do you want?" came the voice from behind an unopened door. "Excuse me, sir," said the young man, "I'd like to invite you to a seminar on interpersonal communication being held this week at . . . " "You're wasting your time," shot back the voice, "I'm retired!"

What do you suppose he meant by that? Retired? Many people have retired from their full-time jobs, certainly, but they haven't stopped growing or learning or living. Jesus was always prodding men and women to keep the process of growth alive. "Ask! Seek! Knock!" he said. If you don't ask, you won't receive. If you don't seek, you won't find. If you don't knock, the door may remain forever closed.

The fact that you picked up a book on building richer relationships through communication says that your growth process is still alive. Good for you! That places you in the company of those of us who haven't yet retired from the business of growing, because we know we can't afford to.

## FROM THE HEART

As I write this, my six-year-old daughter is going through a privacy phase. In order to keep the family advised of her feelings, she has made two reusable signs which she places for our edification on the door to her room. When she is feeling fiercely private, she posts the sign which reads, "You cannot come in! That is that!" But when in a benevolently private mood, she puts up her nicer sign, "Do not come in. I love you."

Jenny is in the midst of that vital process of learning how to communicate what's on her mind and what's on her heart. She's letting the world know where she stands (and where she would prefer that the rest of us stand). But then, that's a lifelong enterprise, isn't it—communicating the unique viewpoint each of us has. After all, nobody else who's ever lived on this planet sees God's creation and creatures in exactly the way you do. So the rest of us need to get your point of view!

And yet, we live in a world that seems already oversaturated with messages and words. "Words, words, words—there isn't one I haven't heard!" complains a weary Eliza Doolittle in *My Fair Lady*. Joyful words, sad words, shy words, arrogant words, healing words, painful words, pious words, profane words—we spend most of our waking hours trying either to take a thought and "put it into words" or to make sense out of the words of others. Some days it's a victory just to get a word in edgewise.

The almost one million words in the English language make up a verbal stockpile, from which we can pull out both tools for building and understanding and weapons for destroying and deceiving. "The tongue," Solomon observed long ago, "has the power of life and death."

But communication is an *inside-out* process. Our words, tone of voice, and body language are outer expressions of our inner selves. So a biblical study of how to build richer relationships through communication—which this book is intended to be—will need to probe much deeper than mere word-level. We'll need to look at what's going on in the primary speech organ.

Jesus says, "The words that the mouth utters come from the overflowing of the heart." (Luke 6:45, NEB). The primary speech organ, the birthplace of our words, according to the Son of God, is the human *heart*. Deep down within our values, beliefs, and convictions—that's where the words come from. If that is so, then our words may be clearer windows into our character than we like to admit. Maybe it's true what the old children's rhyme says: "Twinkle, twinkle, little star. What you say is what you are."

## Communication: The State of the Art

A few years ago I visited the communication hub of one of the world's largest international airlines. In that huge room, computer terminals, teletype machines, and telephone hookups reported the immediate status of hundreds of planes all over the world, in the air or on the ground.

The capabilities of modern communication technology are staggering, almost magical. We have come so far so fast. When my grandparents were born, the Wright brothers still had their feet on the ground. It wasn't so many years ago that folks had to wait days to find out who had won the presidential election; today the winner is announced before all the polls have closed! From my easy chair I can watch a televised tennis match in Australia or talk with a friend in Israel. Incredibly sophisticated communication networks have helped shrink our world down to what Marshall McLuhan has called "the global village."

But where is our technological genius getting us? Are we making better sense to one another, sharing our needs and dreams more honestly? Has our twentieth-century sophistication enabled us to speak from our hearts more sincerely than our ancestors did? Or are there just as many communication gaps, half-truths, and verbal smokescreens today as ever before?

Alexander Solzhenitsyn spoke the truth when he said to a Harvard audience in 1978, "All the glorified technological achievements of Progress, including the conquest of outer space, do not redeem the twentieth century's moral poverty."[1] No, technology has not and will never be our Redeemer. A true Redeemer must be able to transform the heart. And here's good news—such a Redeemer lives! He is the very Son of him who created both heart and tongue.

As we begin our biblical study of the tremendous possibilities for redeemed communication, let's go first to the first chapter of Genesis and begin at the Beginning.

## IN THE BEGINNING

The Bible opens by introducing God to us as the Divine Communicator. History begins as the deep, dark void is shattered when the Creator *speaks:* "Let there be light!" (Gen. 1:3). Order and beauty emerge from chaos as God continues to speak. All living things are *spoken* into being, and they are all "good." And as God creates, he *names* his wonders: "day," "night," "sky," "land," "seas," and climactically, "man."

One of Adam's first assignments is to exercise his God-given ability to communicate. God brings the animals to him "to see what he would name them; and whatever the man called each living creature, that was its name." Names were chosen with great care in the ancient world, because the name expressed the essence of the person, place or thing it stood for. When God asks Adam to name the animals, he is most likely encouraging the man to study and understand the creatures, not just label them. From the beginning, language and understanding have gone hand in hand.

God's crowning act of creation underscores man's essential identity as a communicator. "It is not good for the man to be alone," says the Creator. "I will make a helper suitable for him" (Gen. 2:18). The human communication cycle is incomplete. What is a speaker without a listener? And how can we listen unless someone speaks? Man alone, God dramatically announces, is "not good." So he creates woman.

### God's Most Eloquent Word

Another great communicator was present in the beginning, though his identity was not to be revealed for centuries. "In the beginning," writes John, "was *the Word,* and the Word was with

God, and the Word was God" (John 1:1). Now, when John uses the Greek term *logos* ("word") to refer to Jesus, what is he wanting to tell us?

Today we use "word" to refer to a basic unit of sound or expression. But to the ancient Greeks, the concept of *logos* was much bigger. They used it to describe the very existence of reason and communication in the universe. According to their Stoic philosophers, the *logos* was the powerful but impersonal Force that created and ordered the world. But in the first century, people called Christians were heard making a stunning claim: "The Word [Logos] has become flesh!" (John 1:14). Could it be? The Word—always thought to be so distant, so indifferent to the lives and needs of mere mortals—had become a man? Could it really be that the Intelligence that formed us and the world around us had actually become one of us?

Yes, indeed! Paul testifies of Jesus: "For by him all things were created . . . in him all things hold together" (Col. 1:16, 17). This Word was sent by God as both message and messenger: "In the past God spoke to our forefathers through the prophets at many times and in various ways, but in these last days he has spoken to us by his Son, whom he appointed heir of all things, and through whom he made the universe" (Heb. 1:1-2).

The news of the Word-made-flesh was an absolute bombshell to the world of twenty centuries ago. But it is no less so today.

In our word-saturated world so many of the messages we hear are meaningless, contradictory, or absurd. Confusing images are everywhere. In an ad for a fattening dessert, a slim girl in an exercise suit invites us to an "exercise in indulgence." A billboard shows healthy, happy young people enjoying life and a smoke together, and at the same time issues the warning, "Look out, this could kill you!" "Life" is a breakfast cereal. "True" is a cigarette. "Joy" is a dishwashing detergent.

Eastern religion often presents God as unknowable. But in Jesus, the Living Word, God invites us to know and to understand him. He has revealed himself to us in the most personal fashion possible—man to man—through his own Son. His message to us was never intended to be mystical or ambiguous, but sensible and comprehensible. God wants us to understand.

## When Sin Infects Communication

The ability to communicate with God and with each other is one of the Father's richest gifts. But our sinfulness can garble that gift. When sin first pierces the perfection of Eden, the communication process immediately begins to break down. Adam and Eve disobey God. God comes to speak to them. They hide from him. When discovered, Adam shifts the blame to Eve (even implicating God!): "The woman you put here with me—she gave me some fruit from the tree, and I ate it." Then Eve blames the serpent!

Hiddenness. Evasiveness. Accusations. Haven't we all experienced the same communication breakdown? Burdened by the guilt of unconfessed sin, we don't want to speak to or listen to God. We find ourselves using defensive language, trying to wriggle off the hook of responsibility.

Repeatedly through Genesis, we see sin infecting communication. Cain murders his brother Abel, then lies to God (Gen. 4). Men build the Tower of Babel as a monument to their egos, so God confuses their language (Gen. 11). Joseph's brothers sell him into slavery, then deceive their father Jacob into thinking Joseph was accidently killed (Gen. 37).

Jesus rightly identifies the heart as the birthplace of our words (Luke 6:45). So words cannot be passed off as insignificant ("Oh, that was no big deal—just something I said."), for they reveal what's inside us. Our sin creates alienation from the Father and from one another. We can hear the language of alienation in falsehood and unkindness and profanity and sometimes in the inability or unwillingness to communicate at all. The despair of modern loneliness and noncommunication is captured frighteningly well by Paul Simon: "And in the naked light I saw ten thousand people, maybe more—people talking without

**66**

*The primary speech organ,*
*the birthplace of our words,*
*is the human heart.*

**99**

speaking, people hearing without listening . . . No one dared disturb the sound of silence."

## Who's Responsible?

Most great gifts carry with them great responsibility. So we should not be surprised to learn that the God who has given us the miraculous capacity to speak holds us accountable for how we use it (Matt. 12:36-37).

Helmut Thielicke, who witnessed the atrocities of World War II in his German homeland, said of words and accountability:

> Just think of all the driveling words that are spoken, written, affirmed in lovers' oaths and never kept, hissed in hatred and later rued. Think of the words that fly from mouth to mouth on the gray wings of rumor, all quite anonymous and nobody responsible. Think of the thousands of "Heil Hitlers" that have thickened the air, and the thousands who disassociated themselves from it all with the lame excuse that it was a word without content, an empty matter of form. The question is, however, whether the Last Judgment will take the same view.[2]

Whenever we are tempted to minimize the significance of our words or our accountability to God for how we use them, we would do well to remember the verbal integrity of so many early Christians. "Make your incense offering to the genius of Rome," they were commanded, "and recite these words: 'Caesar is Lord.' " But they would not. They went to prison, even to death, with these words instead on their lips: *"Jesus is Lord."*

## SINS OF THE TONGUE

The New Testament has much to say about the ways we can abuse the gift of speech. The following terms identify the "sins of the tongue":

*Angry talk*—words uttered in a fit of temper; a sudden outburst of wrathful speech (2 Cor. 12:20, Col. 3:8).

*Boasting, arrogant talk*—bragging; conceited, self-centered, self-glorifying speech (2 Tim. 3:2, Jas. 4:16).

*Blasphemy*—speaking contemptuously of God or of Jesus Christ (1 Tim. 1:20, 6:1).

*Coarse joking*—vulgar humor; particularly, the mocking of human sexuality (Eph. 5:4).

*Deception, distortion*—mingling the truth with false ideas or unworthy motivations; Paul spoke of some who "peddled" God's Word, corrupting the gospel for personal gain or advantage (2 Cor. 2:17, 4:2).

*Flattery*—excessive or untrue praise; insincere complimenting of another to gain some personal advantage (1 Thess. 2:5, Jude 16).

*Godless chatter*—profane and empty babbling; conversation which is irreligious, misleading, or worthless (1 Tim. 6:20, 2 Tim. 2:16).

*Gossip*—spreading idle talk, rumor, or personal information about others; betraying a confidence (2 Cor. 12:20, 1 Tim. 5:13).

*Lying*—making false statements with intent to deceive or mislead (Acts 5:4, Col. 3:9).

*Obscenity*—using profane or vulgar language; unwholesome conversation (Eph. 5:4, Col. 3:8).

*Quarreling*—heated verbal strife; unkind argumentation or debate (1 Cor. 3:3, 2 Tim. 2:23-24).

*Slander*—damaging someone's reputation by speaking malicious or untrue things about them (Eph. 4:31, Jas. 4:11).

The common effect of all the sins of the tongue is destruction. Speech infected by sin destroys truth, destroys trust, destroys reputation, destroys love, and destroys respect for God and man. Yet the abuses of language listed above are commonplace in our offices, around our neighborhoods, on our campuses, and even within our churches. We need someone to redeem our speech, to tame our tongues.

### Taming the Tongue (Jas. 3:3-12)

Do you feel like your tongue sometimes has a mind of its own? All of us have made embarrassing slips of the lip, like the famous announcer who introduced Herbert Hoover as "Hoobert Heever," or the television host who misidentified his sponsor General Foods as "General Fools."

But in his book of practical Christian wisdom, James uses strong language to picture the tongue that is willfully out of control: "The tongue also is a fire, a world of evil among the parts of the body. It corrupts the whole person, sets the whole course of his life on fire, and is itself set on fire by hell. All kinds of animals, birds, reptiles and creatures of the sea are being tamed by man, but no man can tame the tongue. It is a restless evil, full of deadly poison (Jas. 3:6-8).

We mustn't be naive about the destructive potential of the tongue. Like the small rudder of a ship, bit of a horse, or spark of fire, the power of a small tongue can be easily underestimated. The rabbis used to say that the tongue is more dangerous than the hand: the hand kills only at close range, while the tongue can kill at great distance.

James' colorful images continue to drive home the point of the tongue's power. When a horse's mouth is controlled with a bit, the horse itself can be controlled and guided: control the mouth, control the life. Just as a small spark can touch off a great fire, a few evil words can spread uncontrollably and yield hellish destruction. Man can tame the great creatures but not his own tongue. Only God can successfully master man and his tongue.

Sometimes we can be guilty of glaring contradiction, like the man who said, "I'd give my right arm to be ambidextrous." James wants to know how can we praise God in one breath, then curse a person made in God's likeness in the next? "Can both fresh water and salt water flow from the same spring" (3:11)? Pious words on Sunday don't offset the gossip on Monday, the profanity on Tuesday, and the harsh words on Wednesday. "If anyone says, 'I love God,' yet hates his brother," John writes bluntly, "he is a liar" (1 John 4:20).

## WISDOM FOR TODAY

The ancient book of Proverbs abounds with very contemporary wisdom about words—their use and abuse, their power for good and evil. The sages of Israel clearly assumed that man was created to communicate, and to communicate honestly, thoughtfully and sensitively.

For the person who doubts the destructive power of words, who would argue, "It's only words," Proverbs replies:

- ☐ "With his mouth the godless destroys his neighbor" (11:9).
- ☐ "Reckless words pierce like a sword" (12:18).
- ☐ "A harsh word stirs up anger" (15:1).
- ☐ "A deceitful tongue crushes the spirit" (15:4).

We used to chant as children, "Sticks and stones may break my bones, but names can never hurt me." But we knew better even then, didn't we? "Chicken," "Sissy," "Fatso," "Four-eyes"—the names cut so deeply; they "pierced like a sword." Then as we grew up, we discovered the more subtle and devastating means of inflicting pain with words—the politely worded put-down, the well-placed bit of gossip, the sarcastic come-back. We found that a human being could be written off with a single stroke of the tongue like "redneck" or "hypocrite" or "liberal." And who can begin to calculate the magnitude of rejection invested in a word such as "nigger"? Sometimes like a scalpel, sometimes like a blunt club, our words can pierce, crush, and destroy. Words are powerful.

But our words can work wonderful good as well. For the person who says, "I don't have anything of value to say to anyone," Proverbs counters:

- ☐ "The lips of the righteous nourish many" (10:21).

☐   "The tongue of the wise brings healing"
     (12:18).

☐   "A gentle answer turns away wrath" (15:1).

☐   "Pleasant words are a honeycomb, sweet to
     the soul and healing to the bones" (16:24).

Do you recognize the power you possess to strengthen
another person with the simple words, "Good job!"? To heal
another with "I'm sorry. Forgive me."? To energize another with
"I love you."? Words don't have to be eloquent or multisyllabic
to be life-changing, if they are from the heart. Words are powerful.

We were created to communicate, and to do so constructively and lovingly. But sin, when it infects our communication,
unleashes its destructive potential. No man can tame the tongue.
But the tongue must be tamed, mustn't it? Otherwise, unharnessed
and out of control, it will injure both its possessor and its victims.
For the redemption that tames the lips and transforms the heart,
we turn to Jesus, God's Living Word. For in him we are re-
created to communicate—re-created in him to communicate like
him.

[1]Alexander Solzhenitsyn, "The Exhausted West," *Harvard Magazine* (July-
August, 1978), p. 26.
[2]Helmut Thielicke, *Life Can Begin Again* (Philadelphia: Fortress Press,
1963), pp. 50-51.

# 2

# *The New Body Language*

Growing up in a faithful, church-going family, I often wondered as a child, what is a Christian supposed to *sound* like? I suppose my earliest communication classroom was the church. The power of words was first impressed on me in Sunday worship, as scriptures, hymns, prayers, and sermons evoked vivid and wonderful mind-pictures—of Jehovah the King of Glory and Jesus the Good Shepherd, of Christian soldiers, of the Church victorious, and of a wondrous place called heaven.

My early struggle to understand the Christian vocabulary was not without its confusing moments, however. I joined in enthusiastically on the rousing song "Bringing in the Sheaves" because I thought we were bringing in the cheese. I thought for the longest time that the old invitation hymn which went, "Sad, sad, that bitter wail—'Almost, but lost' " was about some misplaced and miserable fish. And just who were those disagreeable folks we were always praying for: "those sick of the church"?

## Body Language

What *is* a Christian supposed to sound like? Put that another way: What does God ask of our communication? What does he who spoke the galaxies into being, he who across the centuries

23

has communicated so faithfully and so clearly, expect of our daily speech?

As we try to answer that crucial question, let's borrow and adapt the familiar expression "body language." Normally it describes how we express ourselves in ways other than words— such as gestures, facial expressions, and posture. But could we also use that expression to refer to God's standards of language for his people? The apostle Paul often describes Christians as "the body of Christ." Is there then a distinctive "body language" that Christians are supposed to speak? Are we supposed to sound different from non-Christians? If so, how?

Peter calls the disciples of Jesus "a peculiar people" (1 Pet. 2:9, KJV). He warns Christians to expect to have their values and lifestyle considered strange or unfashionable when measured by the prevailing cultural norms (1 Pet. 4:4). But then, there have always been some religious folk who seem to work hard at looking and acting peculiar for peculiarity's sake. Sometimes they adopt, as a visible mark of their faith, odd clothing styles or bizarre customs or even strange speech. But is that what Peter means by "peculiar"?

In Kentucky there is a lush green grass called bluegrass, which is peculiar to—especially belongs to, is characteristic of— that state. Here is Peter's meaning. Christians are a race of people *peculiar to God*, "a people belonging to God" (1 Pet. 2:9). And as such, their lives and speech should have a distinctively godly character.

God wants to lift our eyes to the highest planes of human values and behavior, to a lifestyle distinctive in quality from our secular surroundings. In Mark 10:43 Jesus points to the value system of pagan society and says to his followers, "Not so with you." Later Paul would warn the church that the world must not be allowed to set her behavior patterns (Rom. 12:2) or shape her point of view (2 Cor. 5:16). The message is clear: God's standards—for our words and deeds—will at times call us to walk a path different from the world around us. But where do we find that standard?

## In Search of a Standard

Every morning the man would pause in front of the watchmaker's shop, gaze at the large clock in the window, set his watch by it and walk on. Every day at noon, the watchmaker would go to the big clock in his window, and set it precisely by the blowing of the noon whistle at the local factory. After many years had passed, the watchmaker stopped the man one day and complimented him on his faithful commitment to the correct time. "Oh, I have to be correct," said the man, "You see, I'm the one responsible for blowing the noon whistle at the local factory." Without knowing it, they had both been using the other as the standard!

Do we use the speech of the people around us as the standard for our communication? That can be risky business. In his book *Christ and the Media*, Malcomb Muggeridge asks us to imagine that, centuries from now, a collection of twentieth-century video tapes are discovered in a cave somewhere. (He calls them the Dead Sea Video Tapes.) Tapes of our television programs, movies, news footage, popular music, and advertisements have been preserved for future archaeologists to study. Based on that evidence, Muggeridge wonders, what would they make of us? Does that question depress you as much as it does me?

Alvin Toffler has written that we are a society with "value vertigo," morally out of balance. Solzhenitsyn says that we have lost the noble quality of moral courage. Where then do we look for absolutes—values that enable us to distinguish right from wrong, essential from dispensable, primary from trivial? Where can we find a reliable, unchanging standard by which to evaluate our communication?

If we look to one another as the standard, like the watchmaker and the whistle-blower, we're in big trouble. We will almost always compound one another's error. But if we look to God and to his Word, we may just find our way past moral relativism to moral courage.

When it comes to healthy, ethical, godly communication, I believe that the standard is to be found in *Jesus of Nazareth*. "Let us fix our eyes on Jesus, the author and perfecter of our faith" (Heb. 12:2). God has provided us with abundant biblical teaching on healthy speech habits (such as Eph. 4:17-5:20 and Col. 3:8-12). But much more than that, he has given us a *living* standard—a man who always spoke from the heart, whose heart was the heart of God. Our standard is Jesus.

Just as Peter's Galilean accent tipped others off that he was one of Jesus' men (Matt. 26:73), so Jesus' followers today must cultivate a distinctive "accent"—one identifiable by its truthfulness, wholesomeness, encouragement, thanksgiving. Yes, there is a body language peculiar to believers. It is the very accent of Jesus Christ, "for we are all members of one body," the Body of Christ (Eph. 4:25).

## New Creation Communication

"If anyone is in Christ, he is a new creation; the old has gone, the new has come!" (2 Cor. 5:17). So what's new in Christ? I like the statement attributed to a Frenchman who had just become a British citizen. "What does your new citizenship mean to you?" he was asked. "It means that I woke up one morning having lost the battle of Waterloo," he answered, "and I went to bed that night having won it!" He was a new person with a new past, present, and future.

A Christian is a man or woman who is being recreated by God, born all over again to live a new kind of life. And one obvious mark of the citizens of Christ's kingdom is their new language. They have a new native tongue. It's an uncommon language of conspicuous quality, remarkably similar to that of the King himself.

One of the primary strategies of this book is to look repeatedly to Jesus as our speech teacher, better yet, our speech *master*. Our objective is to sound like him. No, none of us will ever speak ancient Aramaic with a Galilean accent, but we can and must speak contemporary English with a Christian accent.

**66**

*Body language is not
measured in the quantity
of religious words, but in the
Christ-like quality of our lives that lends
credibility to our words.*

**99**

How do we learn to speak as new men and women? Let's take this approach: First, we admit our need to change our speech. Next we locate the power source for change. Then we ground our communication in a new relationship with God, focus it through a new point of view, and nurture it within a new community.

## The Problem of Unclean Lips

"Woe to me! I am ruined! For I am a man of unclean lips, and I live among a people of unclean lips, and my eyes have seen the King, the Lord Almighty" (Isa. 6:5). When Isaiah stood before God, his most painful awareness seems to have been of the unworthiness of his speech, and that of his people. He knew, long before Jesus confirmed it, that impurity of speech betrays impurity of heart (Luke 6:45).

Reinhold Niebuhr observed that no evidence to the contrary ever seems to disturb modern man's good opinion of himself. Yet Isaiah speaks for us all. Before our holy God, we must admit to unclean lips. We have all sinned and fallen short of his glory (Rom. 3:23).

"Talk is cheap," they say. But who cheapened it? Our ability to speak is a priceless and irreplaceable gift from the Father. (Do you remember the utter frustration and helplessness of your last bout with laryngitis?) We have found too many ways not only to cheapen talk, but also to turn it into a weapon of savage destructiveness. Jesus warns us of the consequences of abusing God's gift: "But I tell you that men will have to give account on the day of judgment for every careless word they have spoken. For by your words you will be acquitted, and by your words you will be condemned" (Matt. 12:36-37).

The careless communicator has been compared to a careless surgeon. Picture a hack doctor who, having given little forethought or preparation to an operation, plunges in with an unsterile scalpel, cutting roughly with no concern for neighboring tissue or later infection.

We have all wielded that careless scalpel: harsh words,

hasty words, proud words, dishonest words, words that erect barriers and tear down bridges, words that stir anger and crush the spirit. For these words and more, you and I can only plead, "Guilty."

Three support groups use our church building each week. One is for people struggling with alcohol, one for people struggling with cocaine, and one for people struggling with irresponsible sexual behavior. Each group insists that no change, no healing, will take place until the person first accepts that he has a problem, and that he needs help from a power above and beyond himself in order to change. Before we can speak with the accent of Christ, we must begin with this confession before God: Our lips are unclean.

## The Power to Change

Bertrand Russell, a lifelong agnostic, wrote, "Man still has a caveman's heart. We must find a way to change the caveman's heart." But how do you change a human heart?

Someone has estimated that there are currently available approximately three thousand diet books, two thousand self-improvement books, and over one thousand sex manuals. Columnist George Will writes of "hundreds of profoundly sad books on achieving happiness." All too often the human formula for personal reformation amounts to little more than "Love yourself. Look out for number one. Think, act, and speak more confidently. Diet, jog and have more fun."

But it is the cruelest of hoaxes to promise a person that he can change, then point him to an inadequate power source or no power source at all. You cannot change the caveman's heart simply by telling the caveman to look inside (or only at the outside) and love what he sees there. You must point him to someone more powerful than himself and to a standard more trustworthy than another person. You point him to the One who not only created him but wants to re-create him as well. You point him to God and to "his incomparably great power for us who believe, the very same power that raised Jesus from the dead" (Eph. 1:19-20).

That brings us back to Isaiah. Left with the guilt of our unclean lips, our final lament would be his: "Woe to me! I am ruined!" But his story doesn't end in despair, and neither must ours. In a dramatic scene, an angelic figure brings from the altar of God a burning coal, and with it purifies Isaiah's unclean lips. "See, this has touched your lips;" he is told, "your guilt is taken away and your sin atoned for" (Isa. 6:7). The grace of God won the day! And now that Isaiah is a forgiven man, he is ready to go out and speak God's word to the people.

What do you do with unclean lips? You confess the uncleanness, to yourself and to God, then you submit yourself to him for his powerful cleansing (1 John 1:7-9).

## THE NEW RELATIONSHIP

An open and healthy relationship between communicators is the soundest basis for effective communication. Relationship and communication go hand in hand. As one grows and deepens, the other grows and deepens. But the reverse is also true— as one suffers and breaks down, the other suffers and breaks down. The Bible says that by our sin we break our relationship with God and build a barrier between ourselves and him, but in Christ that "dividing wall of hostility" is destroyed (Eph. 2:14).

Imagine that a deep ravine separates where you live from where I live. The only way we have of reaching one another is a bridge across the ravine. But I get mad at you one day and burn down the bridge, cutting off contact between us. Sometime later I look out and discover that you are rebuilding the bridge! You, the innocent party, are making it possible for us to be in relationship again.

That's precisely what God did for us through Christ: the righteous rebuilt the bridge to the unrighteous. The biblical word for that action is *reconciliation*, the restoring of a broken relationship.

The Berlin Wall is surely the world's most recognizable

symbol of the barriers people erect between themselves. Between the barbed wire fences that form one of the sections of that hostile Wall stands, of all things, a church building. It bears an ironic name: The Church of Reconciliation. It stands empty, mute, and powerless.

That German church building is a chilling parable of faithless religion. God designed his Son's community to be an authentic "church of reconciliation" in every age and society. Everywhere about us we hear the sounds of "irreconcilable differences"—between mates, family members, friends, business associates, church leaders, heads of state. Christians are called to be the world's salt and light (Matt. 5: 13-14), the bridge-builders and the barrier-busters. As such we must lead the way in the building and rebuilding of richer relationships—between man and man, and between man and God. As Christ's ambassadors, we have a mission and message of peace: "Be reconciled to God" (2 Cor. 5:19-20).

## The New Point of View

We speak to others pretty much according to how we see them. If you view someone respectfully, you'll probably speak to him respectfully. If you see him as an enemy, you may speak to him spitefully. If you see him as unimportant, you may not choose to speak to him at all.

How did Jesus look at people? That's an important question, because in Christ we are to see people from a new point of view (2 Cor. 5:16). Let's attempt to capture Jesus' point of view through an encounter recorded in John 8: 1-11.

Picture yourself as a Jewish woman in first-century Jerusalem, caught up in an adulterous affair. One day you are with your lover, when suddenly the door bursts open. Men drag you out of bed, through the streets, and into the temple court to face a judge. The shame you feel is beyond description. You wish you could die, and well you may, for such is the old law's penalty for adultery.

But what is happening here? You hear the judge talking to

your self-righteous accusers about *their* sins, not yours. Then they begin to leave, until now only you and the judge remain. He stands up and looks you in the eye.

There is something very different in the way this man looks at you. None of that cold, judgmental look you get from the Pharisees; none of that demeaning, lustful look you get from men in the marketplace; not even the vacant, indifferent look most men give you because you are "only a woman." No, this man looks at you differently—with concern, with compassion, even with pain for your humiliation. His gaze somehow grants you dignity, even in this most undignified circumstance. Unspoken words of acceptance.

Finally he speaks: "Has no one condemned you?"

Not quite believing it you say, "No one, sir."

"Then neither do I. You may go." Words of grace. But as you turn to leave, he adds, "You know, you don't have to live that way. Leave your sinful way of living, won't you?" Words of guidance.

We do not know if she left her sinful way or not, but this much we do know: She never had a better opportunity to change than on that day when she encountered a man who did not see her from a worldly point of view. The religious establishment saw her as just another sinner, a dispensable pawn in their religious game. But Jesus saw her as a unique being formed in his Father's image, deserving of respect and grace and a second chance. And when he spoke to her, he communicated both mercy and high expectation.

What did Jesus *see* in people—in the weeping woman (Luke 7), in Zacchaeus (Luke 19), in the woman at the well (John 4), in the man born blind (John 9)—that few had bothered to see before? Why did his words have a credibility and an impact like no one else's? Only by a careful study of Matthew, Mark, Luke, and John can we begin to answer that question. Only as we search for and discover "the mind of Christ" (1 Cor. 2:16) in scripture will we begin to develop his point of view and hear his accents echoing in our own speech.

## A New Community

It is hardly accidental that our words "communicate," "communion," and "community" all sound alike; they're all derived from the Latin word *communis*, meaning "common" or "shared." So the word "communicate" suggests what God intends for us to do with this precious gift: share ourselves with others, experience common life (which is what the New Testament calls "fellowship").

In Christ we are privileged to share our lives in a unique way with other believers who have been baptized into the one body (1 Cor. 12:13). But it's a privilege easily taken for granted. Dietrich Bonhoeffer, who would spend the last years of his life in the isolation of German prison camps, begged the believer not to take Christian fellowship casually: "Let him thank God on his knees and declare: It is grace, nothing but grace, that we are allowed to live in community with Christian brethren" (*Life Together*).

What then is the "body language" of this new community? Some people seem to think that it's the use of certain religious words and expressions. But body-of-Christ language is much more than a "Hallelujah" or a "Praise the Lord" (as good as those expressions are). The apostle John rebuked some church people who were using phrases such as "I know Jesus," "We are enlightened," and "I love God" as pious clichés which didn't square with their behavior (1 John 2:4, 2:9, 4:20). No, real body language is not measured in the quantity of religious words, but in the Christ-like quality of both our words and the lives that give credibility to our words.

John Chrysostom, a fourth-century preacher, once asked, "If the eye sees a serpent, does it deceive the foot? If the tongue tastes what is bitter, does it deceive the stomach?" He was making a point about the church. Just as the human body relies on the honesty of its internal communication network, so the members of the body of Christ must practice absolute integrity with one another. "Each of you must put off falsehood and speak truthfully to his neighbor," instructs Paul, "for we are all members of one body" (Eph. 4:25).

The church can be a wonderful communication classroom. Within the security of relationships with people who love us and have our eternal good at heart, we can dare to "commune," to share our real selves with others. But as members of one body, we have a profound trust to keep. In casual conversation, in doctrinal discussion, in shared prayer, in admonition and counsel, we must "speak the truth in love" (Eph. 4:15). This is the hallmark of our body language.

## New Speech from a New Heart

For too long the myth has been circulated that old speech habits can't be changed. "I can't help it," some people say, "I've always: been a sarcastic person . . . told little white lies . . . used profanity . . . been a gossip . . . said nasty things when I get mad."

True, old speech habits usually can't be changed with human resources alone. But with the power of God to change the heart, they can! My friend Al, who works in the toughest section of New York City's South Bronx, says he never thought he could reform his language, but since he's become a Christian, he's doing it. My friend Mike, the superintendent, says his way of communicating to his workmen on the construction site has completely changed since he committed his life to Christ. Don't say it can't be done!

In the chapters ahead, we'll be looking at specific areas of communication in which the power of God at work within us can do more than all we might ask or imagine (Eph. 3:20). In the beginning, God created man and woman to communicate powerfully, lovingly, and constructively. In Christ he gives the re-created man and woman assurance of the same magnificent possibility.

# 3

# *To Tell the Truth*

Do you remember the old television show "To Tell the Truth"? Three persons stood before the camera and solemnly declared, "My name is _____." All three claimed to be the same individual. Of course, two were imposters, and their object was to deceive the celebrity panel into thinking they were telling the truth. The more successful their deception, the more money they won! While I doubt this program had any real damaging effect on the moral fiber of America, it does remind us of the games people play with the truth.

Tell the truth now—do you always tell the truth? One study found that many people tell as many as fifty lies a day! Someone came up with a list of the most oft-told lies in our society. Among them: "The check's in the mail." "I was only kidding." "I'll get right on it." "I'm sorry." "I didn't mean to hurt your feelings." And a personal favorite of mine, "No, you didn't wake me up." It's frightening, isn't it, how easily and automatically a lie can spring from our lips.

## TRUTH IN THE FLESH

Jesus characteristically uses a certain expression both in his teaching and his conversation. "Verily, verily," he says. One version translates this expression, "I tell you the truth." Now, that was no idle boast nor simply a nice touch of eloquence—it pointed to a primary objective of Jesus' mission.

In the midst of human confusion and misunderstanding, the Son of God came to tell man the *truth*—the truth about God's grace and judgment, the truth about man's limitations and possibilities. And Jesus alone lived and spoke with such integrity, so embodied the truth of God, that he could make the outlandish claim, "I am the way, and *the truth*, and the life" (John 14:6). He was not just a man who always spoke the truth, which is remarkable enough. Jesus was Truth incarnate, the true Word of God come in the flesh (John 1:14).

Telling the truth has always been God's style, his way of communicating to his creation. He cannot do otherwise. "All your words are true," writes the psalmist. "God must be true," Paul tells the Romans, "though every man living were a liar." If God is always true, and if his Son is his Truth, then doesn't it follow that the communication of his people should "ring true"?

## Whom Do You Trust?

Driving past certain slum neighborhoods in New York City, you see cheery curtains and venetian blinds in many of the windows. But wait! Upon closer examination, you discover that what you are actually seeing are vinyl decals of curtains and blinds placed over the broken windows of abandoned apartments. Some ingenious city official thought the illusory decals would make a good impression on potential real estate investors! It looks good. But it's a deception. So again we learn not to trust everything we see or hear.

Whom do you trust to tell you the truth? The news commentators? The politicians? The ministers? The astrologers? Dear Abby? The fact is, most folks are pretty wary about the trustworthiness of most other folks these days. Why? Probably because they have been burned—disillusioned by the careless or deceptive use of words and promises by others. Many can hear a modern ring to Isaiah's ancient complaint: "Truth is nowhere to be found, and whoever shuns evil becomes a prey."

George Washington, we were told, could not tell a lie. And Honest Abe Lincoln, so the story goes, would walk five miles to return a nickel that wasn't his. But in our time the level of public trust in what we hear from our leaders has eroded. We watch international peace treaties violated as though they meant nothing. What are described to us as "nonagressive" military actions turn out to be violent power plays. And we have become all too familiar with the term "coverup."

Every day advertising beckons to us with slick images and grand promises. But while the celebrity promotes his product, a skeptical little voice within us wonders, "Does he *really* drink that soft drink . . . eat that brand of potato chips . . . use that kind of coffee maker?"

We have grown suspicious, even cynical, because experience tells us not to trust what we hear. So when a serviceman says, "I'll have it for you by Monday," we tend to think, "Wednesday, maybe." A Christian friend of mine who set up repair appointments for a well-known national firm was instructed to promise a service call within two days, even if he knew that his repairmen could not make the call by then.

So, whom do you trust? Where are the "truth-tellers," men and women with integrity of speech and life? A Gallup poll asked people what public institutions they had the most confidence in, and interestingly, they said the churches. They trusted the churches ahead of (in descending order) the banks, the military, the public schools, the newspapers, the Supreme Court, television, organized labor, the Congress, and (last) big business.[1]

The churches are trusted. That is encouraging! But what about individual church members? What about you? Is your speech deserving of trust? Is your daily personal conversation distinctively Christ-like in its honesty? John said that Jesus was "full of grace and truth" (John 1:14). If I wear the name of Christ, perhaps I should ask if I also am "grace-full" and "truth-full."

## Letting Your Yes Be Yes

In the Sermon on the Mount, Jesus set forth a principle that should undergird all Christian communication:

> " 'Again, you have heard that it was said to the people long ago, "Do not break your oath, but keep the oaths you have made to the Lord." But I tell you, Do not swear at all: either by heaven, for it is God's throne; or by the earth, for it is his footstool; or by Jerusalem, for it is the city of the great King. And do not swear by your head, for you cannot make even one hair white or black. Simply let your "Yes" be "Yes," and your "No," "No"; anything beyond this comes from the evil one.' "

> (Matt. 5:33-37)

The issue raised here by Jesus is simply this: Does your word stand alone as good or not? A. M. Hunter wrote that "oaths arise because men are so often liars." The need for an oath presumes that there are two kinds of statements—one, backed up by an oath, which is to be believed; and the other, with no oath attached, which should not necessarily be believed. The man who prefaces a statement with an oath, such as "I swear to God . . . " is in a sense saying, "Ordinarily you can't take me at my word, but this time is different."

In first-century Judaism, an elaborate system of rules had evolved as to how oaths should be stated and when they would be binding. The result was, not surprisingly, much ethical hairsplitting. And that made Jesus furious. "Woe to you, blind guides! . . . You blind fools!" he said, lashing out at those religious leaders who made trivial and arbitrary distinctions between binding and nonbinding oaths (Matt. 23:16-22).

A story is told about W. C. Fields, who late in his life was discovered flipping through a Bible. Since this was a most uncharacteristic practice for the crusty comedian, a friend asked what he was up to. Replied Fields, "Looking for loopholes." There was never a more vocal opponent than Jesus of "loophole ethics"—

that legalistic mentality that is always scouting out convenient exits from one's commitments. "Do not swear at all," he says. Why do you need some external form of guarantee? Let your integrity of speech be such that your word stands as its own guarantee. "Simply let your 'Yes' be 'Yes,'" he taught—no hidden meanings, no veiled purposes. Don't play word games that are in reality truth games.

## COMPROMISING OUR STANDARDS

Let's now consider five ways in which we compromise the standards of Christ-like communication, five examples of the yes that is not yes.

1. *Satan's Native Language*

Jesus says of Satan, "When he lies, he speaks his native language, for he is a liar and the father of lies" (John 8:44). The lie is for the Prince of Evil what the truth is for God—his native tongue.

Lying is the most blatant violation of integrity in communication. To lie is to make a false statement with the intention to deceive, or to use words or facts in such a way as to mislead deliberately. Since Adam and Eve first bought Satan's lies, he has used his native language with savage cunning to misdirect human lives. When we lie, in effect, we allow ourselves to become Satan's puppets and him the ventriloquist. Peter's diagnosis of the lie Ananias told about his gift to the church was that Satan had filled his heart (Acts 5:3).

Why do people lie? Pride is always a prime suspect. We lie to create impressions in others that we are more virtuous, responsible, or productive than we really are; we employ lies to cloak our selfish interests, mistakes, or laziness. We defend insensitivity with "I didn't mean to hurt your feelings" or the classic "I was just kidding." Sometimes we lie because we are afraid—afraid to accept responsibility for our words or deeds; afraid to trust others with the truth. Lies are always told in the absence of trust.

It is impossible to exaggerate just how much damage lies

**66**

*Telling the truth has
always been God's style, his way of
communicating to his creation.*

**99**

do to the communication process. Like water in a car's gas tank, lies start a destructive chain reaction. Damage compounds damage, as lie begets lie. I vividly recall the late Senator Sam Ervin of North Carolina shaking his craggy head and reciting at the Watergate hearings the line from Sir Walter Scott, "What a tangled web we weave, when first we practice to deceive."

Solomon wrote, "The Lord detests lying lips, but he delights in men who are truthful" (Prov. 12:22). Truth is for people what a greenhouse is for flowers—the best environment for growth. The lie frustrates God's purposes for us. Human relationships were not designed to work right with deceit and falseness within, any more than a car was designed to run on tap water. Human beings were created for the realm of light, where there is real fellowship and real forgiveness (1 John 1:7), not the realm of darkness, where the language of the Lie is the mother tongue. Nothing is more essential to healthy relationships—between man and God or between man and man—than a climate of trust. And nothing more effectively shatters trust than a lie.

2. *The White Lie*

Most would agree that a "bold-faced lie," the major-league variety, is morally wrong and has no place in the speech of a Christian. But what about that curious species of untruth we call the "white lie"? "Tell him I'm not in," we tell our secretaries when that annoying person calls. Or we encounter the stylish Mrs. Jones in the church lobby: "I love your new hat!" (I hate it.) What about those preachers and other speakers who like to tell a story in the first person (as though it had happened to them personally) to enhance its effect, when in truth they heard it from someone else? And how about the process of exaggeration that expands an insignificant true story into an exciting, grand, untrue one?

What do we do with the white lie? Can Christians accept its use just because it seems to be sanctioned socially? Is it ever harmless to deceive someone? Precisely at what point does a "fib" become a full-fledged lie? If the fundamental assumption of this study is true—that no area of a Christian's speech falls outside the sovereignty of God—then these are troubling questions.

Herman Bezzel writes, "White lies are silken threads that bind us to the Enemy, invisible webs that are woven in hell." One Lilliputian rope tied around Gulliver could never have bound and enslaved him, but hundreds did the trick. The careless use of minifalsehoods in our speech may each in isolation seem innocent enough. But their accumulation can serve only to discredit our words and move us gradually toward the darkness. Our prayer must be, "Keep me from deceitful ways" (Ps. 119:29).

3. *The Empty Promise*

The apostle Paul had opponents in Corinth who apparently accused him of being wishy-washy and undependable, a man who did not honor his commitments. His response was, "Do I make my plans in a worldly manner so that in the same breath I say, 'Yes, yes,' and 'No, no'?" (2 Cor. 1:17). The phrase "in a worldly manner" literally means "according to the flesh" and is an important theme in Paul's letters. He always used it in contrast to the phrase "according to the Spirit," by which he described the life controlled by the Holy Spirit of God. His point to the Corinthians was this: the making of empty or idle promises is characteristic of the worldly man, not the man of God.

When a man's yes is really a no, he is a liar. But what about the man whose yes is almost always a maybe? He makes "good intention" promises: "I'll give you a call" or "I'll take care of it"; but he seldom follows things through. He is consistently fifteen minutes later than he is supposed to be. He often breaks or forgets appointments. He is not devious, just undependable. He makes promises he is not really committed to keeping, and consequently his word slowly but surely loses its credibility among those who know him.

One area in which many Christians are guilty of the empty promise is that of prayer support: "I'll pray for you." Someone shares a private concern with us, or prayer needs are announced to the church family, and we make a mental note to pray about it. But how often do we do so? Most of us are guilty of occasional forgetfulness, but that must not become an excuse for repeated failure to do what we say we will do. The privilege of praying for one another is too important to be taken lightly. Paul makes a special point in his letters to assure his fellow Christians that he is *remembering* them constantly in his prayers (Rom. 1:9-10, Eph. 1:16).

Forgetfulness can be minimized by writing down our commitments. Keep a "prayer list" to prompt your memory. You communicate a special measure of concern and affirmation to a person when you take the time right then and there to make a note of his need. It says to him, "This is no empty promise. You matter to me. I don't want to forget this." The empty promise, like the white lie, seems a little thing. But it serves as an indicator of how seriously we take or fail to take the needs, feelings, and schedules of others. The familiar line from Robert Frost should be our credo: "But I have promises to keep . . . "

### 4. Flattery

Webster defines "flattery" as "excessive, untrue, or insincere praise; exaggerated compliment or attention." We all enjoy a good compliment or a word of praise for a job well done. Christians are to look for ways to encourage each other daily (Heb. 3:13). But the flatterer's sweet, smooth words are but a disguise for his manipulative or selfish intentions.

The Bible speaks out strongly against flattery. "May the Lord cut off all flattering lips," said King David in unusually strong language (Ps. 12:3). Flattery is a grave breach of trust because it, like gossip, is counterfeit caring. I tell you what you want to hear so I can get what I want to have—your preferential treatment, or perhaps just your approval and acceptance. Once again the issue is: Can others trust my words? Is my yes really yes? Paul reassured the Thessalonian Christians that he never used flattery among them, because "we are not trying to please men but God" (1 Thess. 2:4-5).

Flattery is a danger to its object as well. "Whoever flatters his neighbor," says one of the proverbs, "is spreading a net for his feet" (Prov. 29:5). When we listen to pleasant lies, we simply postpone an inevitable confrontation with the often not-so-pleasant truth. Jeremiah blasted the honey-tongued prophets of Israel for prophesying lies of false security to a people who loved to have it so (Jer. 5:31). " 'Peace, peace,' they say, when there is no peace" (Jer. 6:14). Flattery may create the illusion of supportiveness, but "he who rebukes a man will in the end gain more favor than he who has a flattering tongue" (Prov. 29:5).

5. *Honesty in Combat Boots*

"The greatest kindness I have to offer you is always the truth," says John Powell. Honesty is the Christian policy. One of my favorite proverbs says, "An honest answer is like a kiss on the lips" (Prov. 24:26). That needs little exposition! Paul instructs us, "Each of you put off falsehood and speak truthfully to his neighbor, for we are all members of one body" (Eph. 4:25). And yet, the truth can be wielded as a cruel weapon. Have you ever heard a ravaging remark defended by the noble-sounding claim, "Why, I was only being *honest*"? Naked truth without Christ-like compassion is "combat-boot honesty."

Combat boots are thick and tough, providing optimum protection for the wearer, but they can devastate whatever they tread upon. Men use truth wrongly—whether we are talking about the truth of God or simply factual information—when they turn it into combat boots that protect their "rightness" while crushing the spirits of others. Truth is never license for rudeness or insensitivity or arrogance. Many good works and good reputations have been dashed upon the rocks of "truth" by self-righteous religious folk. However factual I may be or however many scripture passages I may quote in my defense, if my speech is at heart unloving, I am just a noisy nothing (1 Cor. 13:2).

As always, Jesus is our finest example. To Nicodemus, "You must be born again" (John 3:7). To the woman at the well, "The fact is, you have had five husbands" (John 4:18). To Peter, "I tell you the truth, before the rooster crows, you will disown me three times" (Matt. 26:34). Honest, straightforward, frank. But never to put himself in a better light, never to inflict pain for pain's sake. When his truth did hurt (as it still does at times), it was the discomfort akin to that of an antiseptic on a wound or of sunlight on eyes that have been in darkness.

## Some Important Questions

Before I tell you "the truth," let me first ask myself:

*What are my motives here?* To put you down? To exalt myself? To "get it off my chest"? Am I concerned more about my honor than yours (Rom. 12:10)? Could I be guilty of dark motives like ambition, conceit, or revenge (Phil. 2:3)?

*Do I have my facts straight?* Are my facts based on first-hand information and reliable sources (Matt. 18:16, 2 Cor. 13:1)? Am I prepared to stand by these facts and accept full responsibility for the accuracy of what I say?

*Is my mind made up and closed shut?* How willing am I to hear another side of the story? Am I determined to "win" this confrontation? Am I prepared to listen and perhaps be corrected (James 1:19)?

*Can I present the truth lovingly?* Am I trying to create as fair and kind an atmosphere as possible? Am I by my verbal or nonverbal signals arousing defensiveness or inviting retaliation? Am I careful to be "slow to speak and slow to become angry" (James 1:19)?

*Does this truth need to be verbalized?* Am I morally bound to express it? Do I have a biblical imperative for speaking out? Would this truth be better left unstated if it has no constructive value (Prov. 17:27)?

Inscribed on a large plaque in the middle of Rockefeller Center in New York City are these words from John D. Rockefeller's personal credo: "I believe in the sacredness of a promise, that a man's word should be as good as his bond, that character—not wealth or power or position—is of supreme worth." Well said. But Paul said it better centuries before:

"Speaking the truth in love, we will in all things grow up into him who is the Head, that is, Christ" (Eph. 4:15).

[1]Princeton Religion Research Center, *Religion in America: 1979-80* (Princeton, N.J., 1981), p. 21.

# 4

# *The Problem of the Grapevine*

One of the first jokes found in the dusty pages of ancient literature goes something like this. One man walks up to another and says, "Hello, friend, I'm surprised to see you. I heard that you were dead!" The other replies, "Well, as you can see, that information is incorrect." The first man says, "I'm not so sure. I heard it from a very reliable source."

While that joke might prove that humor has come a long way since the olden days, it also proves that gossip has been with us for a good while. Gossip. The word itself almost hisses at you, doesn't it?

The bold print on the cover of a popular women's magazine caught my eye the other day. "Gossip is fun!" it announced. That's true, of course. And, that's a major reason gossip has always been such a popular preoccupation. The gossip columnist is a fixture on the American scene. Our seemingly insatiable national appetite for gossip is fed by a host of newspapers and magazines that tattle and tease, spy and speculate, in hot pursuit of the latest choice morsels of news about public and would-be-public figures. *The National Enquirer* claims the largest circulation of any paper in America. Obviously gossip is not only fun, but when properly packaged, highly profitable. The fact is, people love to read and talk about, more than anything else, people.

## WHO IS THE GOSSIP?

The English word "gossip" has an interesting history. Once it referred to a close personal relationship: a dear friend or godparent (thus "god-sib"). But it has come to represent the very abuse or pretense of closeness—the idle talk of a person concerned with the private affairs of others.

In the New Testament, three profiles of the gossip emerge:

*The Busybody.* The busybody, also called the "tattler" (KJV), is the nosy newsmonger who delights in the gathering and spreading of personal information. "The public has a right to know" is his credo. Paul in his writings blames idleness for such behavior: "They are not busy; they are busybodies" (2 Thess. 3:11).

*The Whisperer.* The Whisperer is one who breaks confidences entrusted to him or reveals secrets he has learned about others. Someone else's privacy and trust go right out the window when he whispers, "Now, I probably shouldn't tell you this, but . . . " Proverbs 11:13 says, "A gossip betrays a confidence, but a trustworthy man keeps a secret." Paul associates such gossipy exchanges of information with slander (Rom. 1:29-30).

*The Slanderer.* The slanderer is the most dangerous gossip, for he damages others' reputations by speaking malicious or evil things about them. The terms "back-stabbing" and "character assassination" fit him well, for his intentions are utterly murderous. The Greek word *diabolos* usually refers to "Satan" or "the Devil." But when it applies to a human being, it is translated "slanderer" (1 Tim. 3:11, Tit. 2:3), for that is the literal meaning of the Adversary's name.

## THE INFLAMMATORY GRAPEVINE

Will Rogers observed, "The only time people dislike gossip is when you gossip about *them.*" Have you ever been a victim of the "grapevine"? If so, then you probably can attest that even innocent gossip can grow to dangerous, unforeseen proportions. James' assessment of the tongue's power, "Consider what a great forest is set on fire by a small spark," (Jas. 3:5) clearly applies here.

Not all sparks in the forest touch off fires. But some do. Seven hundred years before Jesus, the Greek poet Hesiod said, "Gossip is mischievous, light and easy to raise, but . . . hard to get rid of. No gossip ever dies away entirely, if many people voice it . . . " Gossip is virtually impossible to exercise strict controls over. Admonitions like, "Now, don't tell a soul . . . " make for pretty cheap and ineffective insurance against its fire.

When I was a kid we sometimes played an old party game called "Gossip." Someone would start a simple message, which was whispered from person to person around the room. After a dozen or so passes, the last person would report the original message as it has come to him. Invariably, the original message has been significantly altered, and we would all laugh at the final product. Not only does gossip tend to live a long life, but it often receives many face-lifts along the way.

The person who is the object of gossip is at a tremendous disadvantage: he usually can't defend himself! For this reason, William Barclay contends that the whisperer is actually worse than the slanderer. "A man can at least defend himself against an open slander, but he is helpless against the secret whisperer who delights in destroying reputations."[1] This abuse is described by the vivid old synonym for gossip—"backbiting"—which suggests a lethal attack from the rear. Jesus demands fair play when one man has a grievance against another: ". . . go and show him his fault, *just between the two of you*" (Matt. 18:15).

## The Damage Done

The Bible condemns gossip in no uncertain terms and shows us the damage gossip can do. Paul in Romans 1:28-32 includes gossip and slander in a potent list of sins characterizing the pagan in rebellion against God. In the midst of other expressions of a "depraved mind" like murder, God-hating, arrogance, and ruthlessness, gossip must rightly be counted as a sin the Christian must view with deadly seriousness.

Why? Because gossip has the potential to damage or destroy two of our most precious personal possessions: our relationships and our reputation.

## Damage to Relationships

Trust is absolutely crucial to a good relationship, be it parental or marital, at work or at church. In *The Friendship Factor*, Dr. Alan McGinnis writes, "One of the signs of deepening friendships is that people trust you with secrets." The more someone entrusts to you his or her real inner self—the fears, the loves, the scars, the dreams—the more vulnerable they become to you.

But vulnerability quickly retreats in the presence of a gossip. An old adage suggests that, "Whoever gossips to you will gossip of you." People who work in office situations—particularly where several desks share the same workspace—often report that the single most discouraging element of their work is the office talk. From outright character attacks to catty speculation about the private details of one another's lives, conversations center on whoever is out of the office at the moment. Such a predatory climate stifles any real kindness, sympathy, or self-disclosure.

It is in such a cultural climate as this that a book with the title *Looking Out For #1* can become a best-seller. Others become the enemy, the competition. Distrust festers. Fear grows. Loneliness deepens. And no one dares share anything from the heart.

## Damage to Reputation

"A good name is more desirable than great riches; to be esteemed is better than silver or gold," says Solomon (Prov. 22:1). In Shakespeare's *Othello*, an agonized Cassio cries, "Reputation, reputation, reputation! O, I have lost my reputation! I have lost the immortal part of myself, and what remains is bestial." Legally, slander is defined as communication by words, gestures, or other signs that seriously damages a person's reputation and thereby exposes him to hatred, contempt, or ridicule.[2]

What value can be placed on our reputation? Like a priceless art object, it deserves to be treated with the greatest care and respect. A good reputation is a necessary quality for an elder of the church (1 Tim. 3:7). But once gossip has let the cat out of the bag, it cannot be retrieved. Excuses, apologies, even complete retractions can never reclaim an errant lie or a broken confidentiality. Gossip writes itself in indelible ink. Some reputations are never able to eradicate its mark; they remain forever tarnished.

Careers, ministries, marriages, even entire congregations of the church have been crippled by loose and unsubstantiated talk allowed to go unchecked because no one had the integrity or courage to break the gossip chain. The terrible effects of gossip are nowhere better described than in the old Jewish proverbs collected by Jesus ben Sirach in *Ecclesiasticus* (around 180 B.C.):

> Curses on the gossip and the tale-bearer!
> For they have been the ruin of many peaceable
> men.
> The talk of a third party has wrecked the lives of
> many
> and driven them from country to country;
> it has destroyed fortified towns
> and demolished the houses of the great.
> The talk of a third party has brought divorce on
> staunch wives
> and deprived them of all they have laboured for.
> Whoever pays heed to it will never again find rest
> or live in peace of mind.
> The lash of a whip raises weals,
> but the lash of a tongue breaks bones.
> Many have been killed by the sword,
> but not so many as by the tongue.

## Gossip's Dark Motives

The Lord didn't place other people on this earth for our entertainment, but for our love. Gossip is a wolfish spirit that often dons the sheep's clothing of loving concern. "Did he really? Poor guy! Tell me more . . . " As the history of the English word suggests, what once was a love for the person becomes twisted into a perverse love for intimate details *about* the person. What are the attitudes that give birth to gossip? Consider these dark motives:

*The Love of Darkness.* Gossip is cheap, cowardly entertainment which almost always zeroes in on the negative, hardly ever the positive. Why does anyone care about Hollywood's latest sexual escapades or Washington's current political scandal? Perhaps Jesus puts his finger on the answer when he says, "This is the verdict: Light has come into the world, but men loved darkness instead of light because their deeds were evil" (John 3:19). The popularity of daytime soap operas (labelled by *Time* as "Sex and Suffering in the Afternoon") and much evening adult programming on television shows clearly that people are entertained by the suffering of others. Perhaps this is the modern day equivalent of the hanging or crucifixion that always seemed to draw a crowd.

"The words of a gossip are like choice morsels;" observed Solomon, "they go down to a man's inmost parts" (Prov. 18:8). Like delicious food, "juicy" gossip begs to be consumed. But just as sexual desire is a God-given appetite that becomes lust when distorted by sin, so gossip appeals to us from the dark side. It is Satan's perversion of compassion. He persuades us to be idly amused by facts that should move us to loving action. An old Jewish proverb says, "To delight in wickedness is to court condemnation, but evil loses its hold on the man who hates gossip."

*Pride.* ". . . Diotrophes, who loves to be first, will have nothing to do with us. So if I come, I will call attention to what he is doing, gossiping maliciously about us" (3 John 9-10). Arrogant Diotrophes became a malicious church gossip. Gossip

**66**

*Gossip has the potential
to damage or destroy two of our
most precious personal possessions:
our relationships and
our reputation.*

**99**

is often rooted in pride. It is a powerful device for discrediting "the competition," if that is how we tend to view others. As John Powell says, "It is much easier to tear down others than lift one's self up by achievement. Superiority and inferiority being relative terms, lowering others seems to raise one's own status."[3]

Another of pride's expressions is the need to be a person "in the know." Privileged information can be treated as a trophy to be displayed: "She confides in me, and the truth of the matter is . . . " By definition, a secret involves information that few know. Flaunting his status as one of the privileged few, the gossip leaks a bit of information just to show others what he knows. But in so doing he violates the true privilege—the privilege of another's trust.

*Guilt.* Gossip can be an attempt to ease a person's feelings of guilt and sinfulness. As we publish the misdeeds of others, we somehow gloss over our own. The name of the game is Comparative Righteousness. Compared to someone else's murderous or adulterous behavior, our mere anger and lust do not seem nearly so serious, hardly worth repenting of. We may feel not only guiltless but even a bit self-righteous. But Jesus did not see it that way (Matt. 5:21-22, 27-28). And Paul warned against the Comparative Righteousness Game: "Each man should test his own actions. Then he can take pride in himself, without comparing himself to somebody else" (Gal. 6:4).

## APPLY THE LOVE TESTS

Authentic Christ-like love *(agapē)* at times necessitates a discreet conversation about someone's personal affairs. Because we are members of the Body of Christ, a brother's sin is *our* concern, a sister's burden *our* burden (Gal. 6:1-2). But we must always take the utmost care to assure that our motives are, in fact, loving. Paul's classic discussion of Christian love in 1 Corinthians 13 serves as the source for the following "Checklist for a Loving Conversation." No gossip can pass these love tests.

In my conversation about this person, have I:

☐  Been kind
☐  Not been envious of them
☐  Not been boastful or proud of myself
☐  Not been rude
☐  Not been self-seeking
☐  Not kept a record of their wrongs
☐  Not delighted in evil facts about them
☐  Rejoiced in their true, good qualities
☐  Protected them and their reputation

At the opposite extreme from the busybody is the one who covers his unloving apathy about others' welfare with the cloak of "minding my own business." A meddler helps no one, but neither does the loveless Christian who always "plays it safe." Gossip only talks. But real love gets involved—sensitively and discreetly in the lives of others. "Dear children, let us not love with words or tongue but with actions and in truth" (1 John 3:18).

## PRUNING THE GRAPEVINE

The gossip grapevine continues to do its lethal damage to reputations and relationships. Its stalk has become thick and strong with popular acceptance. Its roots go deep into our culture's notion of entertainment. But we can prune that grapevine; indeed, we are Bible-bound to do so. Here are some practical suggestions:

*Honor the Individual.* Consider the rights and needs of the person being discussed. Does this conversation need to be *with* him rather than *about* him? Ask: "Does he know that this is being discussed?" Does this conversation honor him; that is, does it have his best interest at heart (Rom. 12:10)? Is there any possibility that he could be misrepresented, betrayed, or slandered by this talk?

*Identify the Source.* Be wary of any personal information which is not firsthand. Ask: "Who told you this?" Reports which begin, "I heard . . . " or, "They say . . . " should not be accepted as satisfactorily documented. If you cannot identify or validate the source of a story, the best policy is not to repeat it. Never report as fact information you are unsure of.

*Guard the Confidential.* If you suspect that you are hearing secret or privileged information, ask, "Should this be kept confidential?" An effective way of both discovering and discouraging a gossip is to inquire, "May I quote you on that?" Don't hesitate to ask questions to clarify the appropriateness of a conversation.

*Resist the Temptation to Pry.* Don't go fishing for more details than you need to know. Seek out only that information about a person's private life that allows you better to bear their burdens and gently restore them to spiritual health and fellowship (Gal. 6:1-2).

*Encourage an Intolerance of Gossip.* Much gossip is aired because people are afraid of offending the whisperer or the busybody. You may first want to try moving the conversation onto more constructive ground: "Now, how can we *help* this person?" Or you may gently suggest, "This doesn't need to be spread any further, does it?" But when subtlety and positive suggestions fail, be straightforward: "This is wrong. This talk must stop right now." Proverbs 26:20 says, "Without wood a fire goes out; without gossip a quarrel dies down." Be a fire-fighter.

*Busy Yourself Serving.* Paul correctly identified idleness as a fertile seedbed for gossip (1 Tim. 5:13). Christians are under the lordship of one who came not to be served, but to serve (Mark 10:45). The more we commit our hearts, minds, and tongues to him and his ministry, the less time and disposition we will have for speech that is irresponsible, careless, or unloving.

The 2100-year-old wisdom of ben Sirach makes for very sound counsel today:

> Confront your friend with the gossip about him; he
>     may not have done it; or if he did it, he will know
>     not to do it again.

> Confront your neighbor; he may not have said it;
> or if he did say it, he will know not to say it
> again.
> Confront your friend; it will often turn out to be
> slander;
> Do not believe everything you hear.

[1]William Barclay, *The Letter to the Romans* (Philadelphia: The Westminster Press, 1975), p. 36.

[2]Carl F. H. Henry, "Slander," *Baker's Dictionary of Christian Ethics* (Grand Rapids: Baker Book House, 1973), p. 625.

[3]John Powell, *Why Am I Afraid to Tell You Who I Am?* (Allen, TX: Argus Communications, 1969), p. 138.

# 5

# *Those Angry Words*

Have you ever noticed how many expressions we have for getting angry? The wealth and color of our anger language suggest what a significant human emotion anger is. We say that we get mad, miffed, irked, irritated, galled, rankled, steamed, frosted, furious, irate, incensed, enraged, exasperated, fed up, put out, and ticked off. Furthermore, we get our danders up, get hot under the collar, lose our cools, blow our tops or our stacks, fly off the handle or into a tizzy, and have conniptions or wall-eyed fits. (It almost makes you mad just thinking about it, doesn't it?)

Word games aside, anger is a sobering matter. Unresolved and unchecked hostility costs friendships, jobs, marriages, and lives. Each year in this country, almost two million wives are beaten, and a million children are physically abused. Over 50% of all homicides involve a victim and assailant who know each other well, and the murder is usually preceded by an angry argument.[1]

How are we to understand and control the rage that sometimes wells up within us? And how do we bridle those hurtful, foolish words that anger so often turns loose?

## What's Going On?

Why do we get angry? Anger is an instinctive response that is touched off when our needs, desires, or goals are somehow frustrated. What should be isn't. Or what shouldn't be is. My world is momentarily out of balance; it has been upset, so I am too.

A lady cuts in front of me in the grocery store line. My boss criticizes my work unfairly . . . or fairly. The vending machine takes my money and gives me nothing in return. A terrorist kills an innocent hostage. Someone makes a cruel, racist remark. Not equally serious offenses, to be sure, but in each my sense of what ought to be has been violated. And my immediate response is to get angry.

As my anger rises, certain physical symptoms predictably appear as my internal system goes on "red alert": more adrenalin is secreted, more sugar is released, my heart beats faster, my blood pressure rises, and the pupils of my eyes dilate. My body is getting me ready for action! In its earliest stages, that's what anger is—the arousal of my mind and body to respond to some perceived threat to my well-being. God made me that way. What I do with my anger, or let it do to me, is another matter.

## Is Anger a Sin?

Does the Bible always equate anger with sin? No. The elder brother in Jesus' parable of the Prodigal Son may have been wrong to get angry (Luke 15:28), but the anger of the king in the parable of the Unmerciful Servant was altogether justified (Matt. 18:34). Jesus teaches that anyone who is angry with his brother will be subject to judgment (Matt. 5:22). But didn't Jesus get very angry at times? And doesn't the Bible describe God as a "God of wrath"?

Paul helps clarify our questions about anger when he cites the ancient wisdom of Psalm 4:4, "In your anger do not sin," (Eph. 4:26). He does not say, "Do not commit the sin of anger." Rather, he makes a clear distinction between the anger that leads to sin and the anger that does not.

A careful examination of scripture reveals that sometimes anger is the *right* response—to injustice, to unkindness, to sin itself. Perhaps you've heard of the group with the angry-sounding name, M.A.D.D. It's an acronym for Mothers Against Drunk Drivers, and their cause is an appropriately angry one. But how are we to distinguish "righteous" anger from "unrighteous" anger?

James writes, "Everyone should be . . . slow to become angry, for man's anger does not bring about the righteous life that God desires" (Jas. 1:19-20). If anger is a response to frustrated goals, then the key question becomes, whose goals are being frustrated—God's or man's? We might define "righteous anger" as that which is directed at the evil that violates the will or righteousness of God. "Unrighteous anger" (what James calls "man's anger"), then, is anger directed at someone or something that is simply failing to meet our selfish desires.

## Righteous Anger: The Wrath of God

Biblical writers often use terms borrowed from human anger—particularly the word "wrath"—to describe God's reaction to sin. The prophet Nahum said:

"Who can withstand his indignation?
Who can endure his fierce anger?
His wrath is poured out like fire;
The rocks are shattered before him."
(Nahum 1:6)

Perhaps the single most famous sermon in American church history is Jonathan Edwards' "Sinners in the Hands of an Angry God," preached in New England in 1741. But it is unfair and inaccurate to cast God as an "angry God" if we are simply picturing him in human terms. For while man's wrath is often impulsive, arbitrary, foolish, and proud, God's wrath is always consistent, just, wise, and righteous. Donald Guthrie defines it as the natural revulsion of absolute holiness to all that is unholy. The wrath of God is his holy displeasure with the sin that wrecks relationships, empties hearts, distorts values, destroys love, wounds the human spirit, and ultimately separates man from the Father.

Actually, God's wrath is good news—because of what he did about it. When we get mad, we often just sit around and stew. Or worse yet, we say or do something destructive. But God's will has never been that we might suffer his wrath, but that we might be saved from it (1 Thess. 5:9). This is our hope in Christ: "But God demonstrates his own love for us in this: While we were yet sinners, Christ died for us. Since we have now been justified by his blood, how much more shall we be saved from God's wrath through him" (Rom. 5:8-9)!

God gave us the very best—his Son—because above all of his qualities stands his gracious, steadfast love. "The Lord is gracious and compassionate, *slow to anger* and rich in love (Ps. 145:8).

## The Anger of Christ

Psychologist Carol Tavris writes in *Anger: The Misunderstood Emotion* that anger is a "moral emotion"; it can be used very rightly and very wrongly. Of justifiable anger she says, "I watch with admiration those who use anger to probe for truth, who challenge and change the complacent injustices of life, who take an unpopular position center stage while others say 'shhhh' from the wings."[2]

Dr. Tavris has just described the anger of Christ. "Consumed with zeal" was a phrase they used to describe him when he made a whip and "cleaned house" at the temple (John 2:13-16). Now, was this a case of man losing his temper and his self-control? Or was his the *right* response to the irreverence he witnessed?

Another day he healed a man's useless hand on the Sabbath. When it became obvious that the Pharisees' traditions were more important to them than the needs and suffering of a hurting person, Jesus "looked around at them in anger . . . deeply distressed at their stubborn hearts" (Mark 3:5). Anger was the *right* response to such callous legalism. (For other examples of his righteous anger, see Matt. 23:1-39 and Mark 10:13-16.) Jesus reminds us that there are times when it is not only right to be angry, but wrong *not* to be!

## Unrighteous Anger: Cain

His is the first birth on record. And the first fit of anger on record. And the first murder on record. His name is Cain, and his story in Genesis 4 is one of unchecked anger. When God preferred Abel's offering to Cain's, "Cain was very angry, and his face was downcast" (4:5). God sees trouble brewing, and questions Cain: "Why are you angry? Why is your face downcast? If you do what is right, will you not be accepted? But if you do not do what is right, sin is crouching at your door; it desires to have you, but you must master it (Gen. 4:6-7)."

But Cain turned a deaf ear to God's warning. His anger turned violent, and he killed his brother. Notice how in Cain we can see many of the same symptoms and dangers of our unrighteous anger:

☐ He became angry out of jealousy and resentment over someone else's success.

☐ He refused to accept responsibility for or learn from his own shortcoming, choosing instead to blame someone else.

☐ He didn't think through his feelings. God asks a key question for any angry person: "Why are you angry?"

☐ He didn't heed God's warning about anger becoming sin: "Sin is crouching at your door; it desires to have you."

☐ He ended up hurting family. Anger often does its worst damage to those whom we are closest to.

☐ He let anger master him, failing to recognize its demonic and destructive potential.

Once again, Satan had successfully seduced man.

## Angry Words

In Edward Albee's wrenching play, *Who's Afraid of Virginia Woolf?*, George and Martha, a middle-aged married couple, spend hours accusing, profaning, and embarrassing one another in front of their guests. In this ugly, painful drama Albee has captured the raw and savage power of angry words.

Good, healthy communication is seldom needed more than when there is anger present. But nothing breaks down good, healthy communication more effectively than anger. All of a sudden, we find ourselves using what semanticist and Senator S. I. Hayakawa called our "snarl-words"—the verbal projectiles we launch at one another in temperamental outbursts.

Why do we "tell one another off," "let them have it," "give them a piece of our mind"? Often, because words are among the most punitive weapons we have available—powerful ammunition with which to punish one another. Rather than an uppercut to the jaw, we give our adversary (often one we care for) what Neil Clark Warren aptly calls "a verbal left and right to the ear." "How could you be so stupid?" "I hate you!" "I'm sorry I ever married you!" And thus, says the old hymn, do our "angry words . . . desolate and mar."

But what we say in anger, and how we deal with anger, is *learned* behavior. And what is learned can be unlearned, corrected, re-created. That is why Paul can bluntly say, "Get rid of all bitterness, rage and anger, brawling and slander, along with every form of malice" (Eph. 4:31). We do not have to be at the mercy of our anger; we can learn how better to deal with it.

## DEALING WITH OUR ANGER

When Paul says, "In your anger do not sin: Do not let the sun go down while you are still angry" (Eph. 4:26), he seems to be saying that anger will often lead us into sin when it is left *unresolved*. People deal with anger in different ways, and some of those ways leave their anger treacherously alive.[3]

**66**

*There are times when
it is not only right to be angry,
but wrong not to be!*

**99**

## Nursing Anger

Sometimes we can deliberately nurse a resentment to keep it alive. We feed it with regular recollections and delight in thoughts of sweet revenge. Or we hold on to an angry grievance as a "pet rock" that we are saving for just the right time to hurl at the object of our anger. Frederick Buechner likens this kind of sinful anger to a savory feast we set for ourselves; but the tragic irony is, "what you are wolfing down is yourself. The skeleton at the feast is you."[4] Unresolved anger can devour our kindness, our patience, our joy, and even our very faith.

When we repress or nurse anger, we not only fail to deal with it, we leave ourselves at its mercy. And when anger deals with us, the results are almost always painful and ugly. When we are angry, evil lies crouching at our door (Gen. 4:7), and unresolved anger gives the evil one a most convenient foothold (Eph. 4:27).

## Suppressing Our Anger

Sometimes the healthiest way to deal with anger is to *suppress* it. When we suppress our anger, we are recognizing the strong emotion within us but keeping it under control. We are not denying our anger; we are managing it. "A fool gives full vent to his anger," observed Solomon, "but a wise man keeps himself under control" (Prov. 29:11).

There is much wisdom in the old counsel, "Bite your tongue!" when we are tempted to verbalize our anger. Consider the advantages. Suppression guards us against silly, unkind, unfair responses made in the haste and heat of the moment. It slows the flow of fuel to our anger and the other person's. It gives us time to reflect: Why am I feeling anger? It gives the other person time to cool off.

A wise friend and fellow minister of mine once counseled me never to "preach mad," that is, with angry feelings still running high. "Make some notes about your feelings and concerns," he told me. "Examine your feelings and what prompted them. Pray. Examine God's word for guidance on a proper response. Pray some more. Then after a few weeks have passed, if you still feel a need to address the concern in a sermon, go to it." His advice has more than once restrained me from delivering a message that would probably have been foolish or unkind or ineffective or all of the above.

Sometimes anger will dissipate and go away. But more times than not, we will need to express it in some way. Suppressing it for a time gives us the chance to consider the kindest and most effective means of expression.

## Repressing Anger

When we repress our anger, we deny that it exists. Some Christians have the notion, "Anger is an illegitimate emotion for nice people. So what I'm feeling can't be anger; I'll just ignore it." But repressed anger does severe internal damage. It has been linked to such physical distress as headaches, hypertension, and ulcers. Bury your anger, it has been said, and it may bury you. When repressed anger goes underground, it often resurfaces in other ways such as depression, sarcasm, or general irritability. When we repress our anger, we minimize the healing of its wounds.

## Expressing Our Anger

There are many advocates today for immediate *expression* or ventilation of anger. "Get that anger off your chest," they counsel. "Vent your spleen. You'll feel so much better when you do." But do we? Does telling someone off while in a state of fury really refresh and fulfill us? Blowing up may carry with it a momentary sense of power and exhilaration, but studies show that many people feel low self-esteem and depression for days after they have spoken angrily to someone. Expression that becomes explosion may achieve some short-term gain, but more often will result in long-term *loss*—of self-esteem, of friendship, of communication.

Expressing anger is no automatic solution to the situation that caused it. In fact, expressing anger while we are still feeling angry nearly always makes us angrier! Furthermore, words uttered in anger are seldom as loving, fair-minded, or well-reasoned as they need to be. "A quick-tempered man displays folly" (Prov. 14:29).

Because anger is such a high-energy state, finding a physical release valve for that energy is often a very healthy form of expression. The best simmering-down activities will vary from person to person. Some people need to clobber a punching bag or jog themselves to exhaustion; others find a quiet game of chess or a Beethoven symphony just as effective.

## Confessing Our Anger

The best strategy for most anger is to *confess* it—to ourselves, to the person we're angry at, and to God.

*To Ourselves.* First things first. We begin by admitting to ourselves that we're angry. (No repressing, please.) When we own up to our anger, we have made the first big step in taking responsibility for it. Accept no rationalizations: "I can't help it, I'm just temperamental" (usually followed by) "because I'm Italian, or Irish, or red-headed . . . " We do not have to be helpless against our anger. The initial response of anger may be instinctive, but sustaining that anger is a decision.

*To the Person We're Angry With.* This confession may not be necessary or even possible. Christian love is "not easily angered" (1 Cor. 13:5). And if it is also patient and kind and not rude and keeps no record of wrongs (13:4-5), then we will often forego the need to report every frustration we feel.

But when our anger needs to be confessed—for our good, or theirs or for the reconciliation of a relationship—let's be straightforward about it. Bearing a grudge only prolongs the frustration. Dishing out our hostility in sarcastic verbal cuts just makes things worse. The biblical mandate is clear: we are to go to the person and talk about it (Matt. 18:15).

But before we do, it's always wise to simmer down first. Then, with our wits about us, we should be able to devise a plan for expressing our feelings as fairly and kindly as possible. We may even discover upon closer and cooler examination that we have a sin to confess to our brother or sister (Jas. 5:16).

*To God.* Sometimes we are tempted to assume, "If it's *my* anger, then it must be *righteous* anger." You know how that goes: When the other guy takes his time, he's being slow; when I do, I'm being careful. When the other guy criticizes, he's being negative; when I do, I'm being discerning.

Prayer offers perhaps the best environment for honestly evaluating our emotions. Present them to God. David did. So did Jeremiah and Job and Amos and Jesus. Bringing our anger into the light of God's presence has a way of clarifying our vision, helping us distinguish what is righteous from what is not. The best cure for unrighteous anger and all the destructive baggage that goes with it is the Father's forgiveness. "If we confess our sins, he is faithful and just and will forgive us our sins and purify us from all unrighteousness" (1 John 1:9).

## BREAKING THE ANGRY-WORD CYCLE

I like to jog at a local high school track, so I enjoyed hearing a middle-aged man's story about his jogging experience. He was puffing around the track that circled the high school football field while the team was practicing. When the players started running their sprints up and down the field, he told himself, "I'll just keep running until they quit." So they ran. And he ran. And they kept running. And he kept running. Finally, in exhaustion he stopped. An equally exhausted football player walked past the jogger and said, "Boy, I'm glad you finally stopped, Mister. Coach told us we had to keep running wind sprints as long as the old guy was jogging!"

Sometimes we find ourselves caught in just such a stalemate when it comes to anger and conflict. Neither side wants to be the first to give in, to stop speaking in anger. They stay mad. So we stay mad. And on we go, eventually finding ourselves emotionally and even physically exhausted by the ongoing animosity.

Have you ever noticed how angry words almost always

provoke more angry words in response? One raised voice is met with another ("Don't shout at me!" "Shouting! Who's shouting!?"). One insult is countered by another ("Who are you calling an idiot, you jerk?") A shouting match never has a winner. Rather than the air being cleared, it is usually left full of the noxious fumes of verbal warfare.

The temptation to retaliate to others' angry words is so strong. Some will advise: "Don't get mad; get even." But Jesus gives some of his strongest and most fundamental teaching on the contrast between Christian response and worldly retaliation. You call your brother "Fool!" in anger at the risk of hell fire, he says (Matt. 5:22). You are not to play the world's retaliation game, he maintains repeatedly (Matt. 5:38-42).

## Turning the Other Cheek

Some have misunderstood the "turn the other cheek" principle. To be slapped with the back of the hand on the right cheek in Jesus' day was to be *insulted*. The Lord is not saying to stand and let someone knock your block off. His message is, don't return insult for insult. If you have to surrender some of your rights to keep an angry person from dragging you down to their level, do so. But you don't slander them in return—turn the other cheek. Break the angry-word cycle.

When Jesus calls us to "love your enemies," he doesn't mean only those engaged in military warfare with us. We are to love everyone, friend and foe alike, while we are angry or at enmity with them. In Luke 6:27-28 he tells us how:

*"Love your enemies."* First, we must make the *decision* to love them. We cannot simply respond to their loveliness, because when someone is mad at us they are usually not very lovable. (Only in the movies do people say, "You know, darling, you're beautiful when you're angry!")

*"Do good to those who hate you."* Deeds of love can put out the fires of anger. Augustine said, "Good for good, evil for evil,

that is natural. Evil for good, that is devilish. But good for evil, that is divine."

*"Bless those who curse you."* Counter the destructive word with a constructive one. Ancient Jewish society had a rich repertoire of curses, such as, "May every tooth in your head fall out but one, and may it have a cavity." Don't get caught up in retaliatory verbal exchanges. Remember the old adage, "When you throw mud, you lose ground."

*"Pray for those who mistreat you."* What better way to guard our attitudes against the bitterness that turns anger into sin, than to talk to God about our adversaries and their needs?

## When You Feel the Heat

Learn the early-warning signals of your anger. Be a student of your own emotional patterns. Think back to the last time you became unrighteously angry: When could you first have seen it coming? Then, when you recognize the first "red flag" of anger building within you, it may be helpful to:

*Count to ten before you respond.* The Roman philosopher Seneca said, "Hesitation is the best cure for anger." Say, if need be, "I'm too worked up to say anything constructive right now. Can we discuss this later when I can give you a fairer response?"

*Hear the other person out.* Determine not to make a rash, premature judgment of them or the situation.

*Use a preselected word,* like "Think" or "Red-Alert" to prompt a mental evaluation of your emotional state. Remember God's question to Cain: "Why are you angry?" You might also ask yourself, "Who am I really angry with?"

*Don't yell back.* "A gentle answer turns away wrath, but a harsh word stirs up anger" (Prov. 15:1). Respond to a loud and angry voice with an even and controlled voice.

*Pray*—for patience, kindness, courtesy, and self-control. Pray for God's forgiveness of unrighteous anger. Pray for the loving spirit of Christ that turns righteous anger into positive energies for justice, servanthood, and love.

¹Neil Clark Warren, *Make Anger Your Ally* (Garden City, NY: Doubleday & Company, Inc., 1983), p. 11.

²Carol Tavris, *Anger: The Misunderstood Emotion* (New York; Simon & Schuster, Inc., 1982), p. 23.

³See discussions by David Augsburger, *The Freedom of Forgiveness* (Chicago: The Moody Press, 1970), pp. 51-72, and H. Norman Wright, *Communication: Key To Your Marriage* (Glendale, CA: G/L Publications, 1974), pp. 87-92.

⁴Frederick Buechner, *Wishful Thinking* (New York: Harper & Row, 1973), p. 2.

# 6

# *Taming the Profane Tongue*

Curseaholics Anonymous was an anti-profanity organization begun in Massachusetts to help people stop swearing. They even offered a 24-hour hotline service. But they received so many foulmouthed calls from irate swearers that they disbanded within a month!

Since about the time Rhett Butler hurled his then-shocking parting line at Scarlett O'Hara in *Gone With the Wind*, the level of profanity has been steadily on the rise in our society. What was once considered the exclusive vocabulary of "washroom poets" now is heard on evening television and in all but the G-rated movies. The obscenities of yesterday's high school locker rooms are now heard on today's grade school playgrounds. What's going on with this increasingly open use of words that shows respect for neither God nor man?

## What Is Profane?

The word *profane* means, literally, "before the temple"; that is, not sacred or reverenced. Thus, to profane is to treat holy things as though they were common and not to be respected. God chastised ancient Jerusalem through his prophet Ezekiel, "Her priests do violence to my law and profane my holy things;

they do not distinguish between the holy and the common" (Ezek. 22:26).

Where do profane words come from? They are typically drawn from those areas of the human experience that are most sacred or intimate. Religion, sexuality, and bodily functions are the objects of almost all profanities. The fact that they are profound and/or personal makes it profane to speak of them without the respect due them. In other words, something has to be valued highly before we can devalue it with profanity.

No word or expression is profane in and of itself. A word is merely a combination of sounds. But people give words their meaning and significance. People make use of certain words— some considered profanities, some not—to degrade, insult, assault, and injure. Anger, contempt, and racism come from our hearts, not from phonetic sound units. The sin of profanity originates where all speech originates: in the human heart.

## Jesus on Profanity

The Master clearly identifies the heart problem behind so much profanity in Matthew 5:21-22. He places verbalized anger and insults in the same league with murder. "Anyone who says to his brother, 'Raca,' is answerable to the Sanhedrin," he says. "But anyone who says, 'You fool!' will be in danger of the fire of hell."

*Raca* was an Aramaic term of insult and contempt, implying stupidity and inferiority.[1] William Barclay characterizes it as a word whose very sound communicates a harsh spirit. Try it: "Raca!" A modern equivalent would be a vicious, "You idiot!" or, "You imbecile!"

Jesus speaks even more critically of *more* ("You fool!"), a Greek expression which insulted not only a man's mind but also pronounced divine judgment on his character.[2] These kinds of words—and particularly the spirit that prompts their use—have no place in his kingdom, Jesus says. To further emphasize the gravity of such verbal behavior, he adds that those who insist on engaging in the regular practice of verbal contempt place themselves in real danger of God's eternal judgment.

## Why Profanity?

I can remember my first curse. I was leaning over the water fountain in third grade. When the water shot up and got me squarely in the eye, I heard a voice strangely like my own exclaim, "Damn!" Who said that? Did I say that? I'd never said that before, but there it was, the sound of it still echoing accusingly in my mind. Luckily, the teacher didn't hear my first four-letter word, but my shame lasted well into the next week.

Throughout history, every culture and language seems to have had its profane words and expressions. Sigmund Freud, in a classic bit of overstatement, suggested that the founder of civilization was the first caveman who hurled a curse instead of a weapon! If I had to choose between the two, I suppose I'd rather be hit with the curse. But do we really need foul language? What purpose does it seem to serve? Here are some of the possible reasons why people use profanity:

*To Communicate Disdain for Authority.* The rhetoric of social protest and political rebellion is often seasoned heavily with profanity. Frequently, profanity is used to communicate defiance. When someone directs a menacing word at an authority figure, such as his parent, teacher, government, or God, he may be attempting to relieve feelings of helplessness, inadequacy, or turmoil.

*To "Blow Off Steam."* Some psychologists consider swearing to be a useful and healthy safety valve for releasing pent-up frustrations and hostilities. "Translate your ugly feelings into ugly words," says this school of thought; "you'll feel better for it." Toward this end, the town of Zurich, Switzerland, provided an obscenity telephone service whereby callers could call in and ventilate their anger by swearing to their hearts' content (for a dollar a minute).

*To Punctuate Conversation.* Profanity is both an effective attention-getter and a proven means of adding color (perhaps

we should say, off-color) and punch to conversation. A well-
timed dirty word raises others' eyebrows and gives the speaker
the momentary spotlight. Profanity has shock-value, because it
is not socially approved. If a profane word had no shock value,
it would carry no color or punch. (As an easy substitute for more
creative or expressive speech, profanity tends to make its users
word-lazy.)

*To Retaliate Against Others.* Profane words can be used like
verbal projectiles tipped with poison. When a person's pride is
wounded or his efforts are frustrated, he will often seek to
retaliate with the closest weapon at hand. Profanity is a potent
and punitive means of communicating disrespect, criticism, dis-
obedience, and condemnation.

*To Gain Social Acceptance.* Children probably begin swearing because they are mimicking forbidden "adult" behavior.
Many men equate profanity with masculinity. A man may toss
into a conversation a strategic obscenity or dirty joke just to
assure his place as "one of the boys." Men and women alike use
expletives in an attempt to demonstrate their adulthood, libera-
tion, or sophistication.

People use profanity for other reasons—to get a laugh, to
offend the prudish, to mock a social taboo, or even to send subtle
seduction signals to a member of the opposite sex.

Now let's look carefully at the major categories of profanity,
and see how they affect the human heart.

## GOD'S NAME IN VAIN: BLASPHEMY

"Holy, holy, holy is the Lord God Almighty, who was, and
is, and is to come" (Rev. 4:8). Holiness is that one attribute of
God which, more than any other, sets him apart, distinguishing
the divine from the mortal, the Creator from the created. " 'To
whom will you compare me? Or who is my equal?' says the Holy
One" (Isa. 40:25). Man's only appropriate response to the Holy
One is reverential awe and worship (Ps. 96:9).

Blasphemy has been defined as dishonoring or mocking the
name, being, or work of God by words or action. The most

blatant profanity is the failure to respect God himself. The third of the Ten Commandments states, "You shall not take the name of the Lord your God in vain" (Ex. 20:7). God's name was considered so holy in ancient Israel that it appeared in written Hebrew as four consonants without vowels (YHWH) so that it would be unpronounceable.

The third commandment probably referred, in particular, to the wrongful use of God's name for evil purposes, such as curses, perjured testimony, or even magic incantations. But its broader application forbade any kind of careless, irreverent usage of his holy name in ordinary conversation.

Jesus identifies blasphemy against the Holy Spirit as what some have called "the unforgiveable sin" (Mark 3:28-30). At issue here is not so much a verbalized oath against the Spirit, as it is a rejection of the authentic power of God. Jesus' enemies were dismissing his power—God's power—as Satan's power. That's moral inversion: calling good evil and evil good. And that's what Jesus considered blasphemous and unforgiveable, for it is the complete anti-God state of mind. How can God forgive the man who doesn't acknowledge God's power to forgive?

"The essential profanity against God," writes Perry Cotham, "is man's dogged refusal to take him seriously" (*Obscenity, Pornography, & Censorship*). An exclamation which has now become a regular feature of many people's working vocabulary is "Oh, my God!" They don't mean anything by it, of course, but that's precisely the problem. They inject God's holy name into the picture, and it means nothing. His majesty, his glory, his awesome power, his unspeakable love—all that the name *God* stands for—are trivialized. Let's ask ourselves: In the final analysis, is it more obscene to curse God than to ignore him?

## DESIGNED TO OFFEND: VULGARITY

The word *vulgar* means common. The *Vulgate* was Jerome's classic Latin translation of the Bible in the fifth century, so named because it was written in the language of the *common* man. Today "vulgar" identifies crude, distasteful, or offensive speech. These are the words that typically refer to urination, excretion, or sexual intercourse. The crime they commit is the crime against good manners.

Paul seems to have this kind of speech in mind when he warns the Colossians, "You must rid yourselves of filthy language" (Col. 3:8). The Greek word he uses refers to obscenities, suggestive expressions, or any talk which betrays impure thinking. He uses a similar term in Ephesians 5:4, warning Christians of "filthiness" (RSV).

The words in our language used to describe elimination and sex are not intrinsically dirty. And yet each society recognizes some words as stronger or more offensive than others. With any words we choose, we must carefully consider the effect they have on others.

For instance, Paul chooses to employ a very strong Greek word, translated "dung" or "excrement," to describe the value of his human accomplishments when compared to the greatness of knowing Jesus as his Lord (Phil. 3:8). Raw, perhaps, but not vulgar. The Song of Solomon in the Old Testament describes the intimacies of sexual love in terms that are sometimes explicit but never vulgar. The Bible is not a prudish book; it often uses strong language to make a strong point.

Vulgar speech is wrong for the simple reason that it *intends* to be vulgar. Its aim is to shock, to offend, to disgust others. Take away the shock of an expletive, and people will stop using it as an expletive.

At best, using vulgarities can be discourteous and insensitive. At worst, vulgar language can (1) indicate an unhealthy preoccupation with sexual sins such as lust, fornication, adultery or incest; (2) foster calloused attitudes towards interpersonal relationships (sexual humor tends to debase women in particular); or (3) express unloving aggressiveness or unbridled hostility.

## CALLING PEOPLE UNCLEAN: RACIAL SLURS

Many Americans laughed at Archie Bunker because he was a foolish and bigoted character. But I suspect many laughed *with* him because he tapped deep reservoirs of prejudice with his constant racial slurs.

Racial slurs often don't get included in discussions of what is profane or obscene. But we use an ungodly double standard when we pronounce certain four-letter words as sinful, then wink at language which demeans a person of another race, or relish a joke that draws its humor from the implied foolishness of a certain ethnic group.

In Acts 10, God makes a dramatic appearance to Peter in a vision to teach him that the church must accept Gentiles as full-fledged brothers and sisters in Christ. Don't miss this fundamental Christian speech principle that God revealed to Peter: "God has shown me that I *should not call any man impure or unclean*" (Acts 10:28).

If we truly want God to cleanse our hearts of destructive and deeply-embedded prejudices, we must rid our language of those terrible words and jokes that call men "unclean." Take the word "nigger." Loaded with racial contempt and arrogance, it degrades human beings made in the image of the God who is neither red nor yellow, black nor white. The language and humor of racial prejudice are always built on the twisted assumption that "we" are inherently better than "they." Hear God's word clearly: "Do nothing out of selfish ambition or vain conceit, but in humility consider others better than yourselves" (Phil. 2:3).

From the overflow of the heart, the mouth speaks. What is in a man's heart when he calls another man a "nigger" or a "honky" or a "Polack" or a "wop" or a "kike"? You can be sure it's not love.

Old speech habits and prejudicial attitudes die hard. But such as these must die. Jesus laid down his life to demolish man-made barriers to fellowship and understanding and to usher in a kingdom where there is "neither Jew nor Greek" (Gal. 3:28). His followers must lead the way in laying aside all racial slurs, unkind ethnic humor, and any other language that slanders people on the basis of their color or nationality.

"With the tongue we praise our Lord and Father, and with it we curse men, who have been made in God's likeness. Out of the same mouth comes praise and cursing. My brothers, this should not be" (Jas. 3:9-10).

## WORDS OF DISRESPECT

There are some additional ways in which we demean others by our speech:

*Sarcasm and Insults.* It's difficult not to relish a clever, well-timed insult. One of the classics is Churchill's response to Lady Astor. She: "Winston, if you were my husband, I should flavor your coffee with poison." He: "Madam, if I were your husband, I should drink it."

I had a great group of friends in college. We considered ourselves to be pretty witty fellows and took great delight in applying verbal scalpels to one another. It became a daily game with us. But in time, what started out as harmless fun began to turn into low blows and cheap shots as we tried to top one another. I well remember the night we all gathered in a dorm room and called a long-overdue truce on the insults.

Both insults and sarcasm are, by their very nature, put-downs. As such, they usually aim for the sensitive and vulnerable areas where a person's weaknesses, failures, fears, and insecurities reside. But the weakness of another should prompt exactly the opposite response from a Christian. "We who are strong ought to bear with the failings of the weak, and not to please ourselves. Each of us should please his neighbor for his good, to build him up" (Rom. 15:1-2).

*Insensitive Humor.* I love a good joke, and, I must confess, I love to pick at and tease my friends. But humor at the expense of someone else is like walking through an old mine field—you can never be absolutely sure you won't trigger a painful explosion. How many people have been ridiculed by someone who was "just kidding"?

In Ephesians 5:3-4, Paul writes that among those sins of the spoken word is "coarse joking." This Greek expression has an interesting history. Among the ancient writers, it was first used as a flattering description of a quick-witted, clever humorist. But later it came to mean, as Paul uses it, wit turned unkind—jesting in an offensive or even cruel way.

When I'm privileged to perform a wedding, I often include in the ceremony this charge to the couple: "Maintain a healthy sense of humor about yourself, but never fail to take the other seriously." Humor is a wonderful way to keep our spirits high and our failures in perspective. But humor, like human beings, must be handled with care. People are the most important thing God put on his earth; the only thing he became one of. We may tease them, poke gentle fun at them, and laugh with them. But we must never ridicule them.

*Labels.* "Good Samaritan" may be a complimentary idiom today, but in the first-century Jewish community it had the discordant sound of shocking contradiction—like "precious garbage" or "lovable terrorist" would sound to us. But Jesus changed all that. He defied the stereotype and forced his listeners to see a person beneath a label.

Another time he asked a Pharisee named Simon, "Do you *see* this *woman*?" (Luke 7:44). Whether he read Simon's heart or just the look in his eyes, Jesus could tell that Simon had already pinned a judgmental label on this penitent person who was washing Jesus' feet with her tears. The label totally obscured the woman, and it read, "Sinner" (Luke 7:39).

An old song asks a question we should all ponder: "In the dungeon of your mind, who've you got chained to the wall?" Jew, Negro, Wasp, Yankee, Southerner, white-collar, blue-collar, senior citizen, teenager, housewife—the list of labels is endless.

People naturally fall into certain categories, of course. But we do not have the mind of Christ when we judge, despise, or ignore them on the basis of those categories. The next time we catch ourselves thinking, "She's just a waitress," or "He's a typical Jew," we need to hear the voice of Jesus asking, "Do you *see* this *woman?* Do you *see* this *man?"*

## TAMING THE PROFANE TONGUE

"No man can tame the tongue," James says (Jas. 3:8). But this is hardly meant to be a biblical escape clause for those who have profane tongues. Perhaps no man can, but God can.

Profanity can be controlled. Most habitual swearers exercise some measure of control—they curse only in certain situations or company. Some men, for example, swear profusely around other men but never around women. One man who learned to quit swearing was the author of the great work *Pilgrim's Progress*, John Bunyan. After giving up profanity, he said, "Now I could speak better and with more pleasantness than ever I could before."

At the heart level, here are four Christ-like attitudes we can pray for and grow in as we learn to control profanity in all its forms—blasphemy, vulgarity, racial slurs, and the rest:

*A Reverence for Our Holy God.* "Just as he who called you is holy, so be holy in all you do" (1 Pet. 1:15). Confronted with the awesome holiness of Jehovah the King of Glory, how can we trivialize or curse his name? And how can we demean one made in his image, one for whom his Son went to a cross?

*A Reverence for Persons.* "From now on we regard no one from a worldly point of view" (2 Cor. 5:16). Any speech that strips human beings of the dignity due them is intolerable. No man should have to bear the indignity of being called "unclean." A racial slur is every bit as obscene as any vulgarity.

*A Concern for Excellence.* Paul's list of worthy Christian standards in Philippians 4:8 provides us with a checklist we can use to evaluate any of our words: Are they noble? Are they pure? Are they lovely? Are they admirable? Are they excellent?

*A Spirit of Thanksgiving.* "Nor should there be obscenity, foolish talk or coarse joking, . . . but rather thanksgiving" (Eph. 5:4). Thanksgiving is profanity's opposite state of mind. When

**66**

*The sin of profanity
originates where all speech originates—
in the human heart.*

**99**

we are speaking joyfully and "in view of God's mercy" (Rom. 12:1), it is difficult to be verbally insensitive, vulgar, or abusive.

The English language, stewarded properly, can be used with great sensitivity, precision, and beauty. Profanity denies the nobility of language and demeans both the user and his object. When we keep the profane tongue in check, we not only discipline our hearts to be kind, we learn to use language more creatively and responsibly.

It's true, we all need a good verbal catharsis at times, an unloading of our internal tensions and hostilities. Even good old Charlie Brown has to let out a "Good grief!" now and again. But we don't have to ridicule our God or the people around us when we do. Our Father is powerful. With his new life within us, we have all the resources we need to communicate our emotions, delete our expletives, and tame our tongues.

[1]T. S. Kepler, "Raca," *The Interpreter's Dictionary of the Bible*, Vol. 4 (Nashville: Abingdon Press, 1962), pp. 3-4.

[2]W. E. Vine, "Fool, Foolish," *An Expository Dictionary of New Testament Words* (Old Tappan, N. J.: Fleming H. Revell, 1940), pp. 113-114.

# 7

# *Beyond the News, Weather, and Sports*

"Good morning, Ken Durham," read the message on the screen of my friendly 24-hour bank machine. "What transaction would you like to make?" I punched the "Deposit" button and entered my secret code number. "Is this the correct code number?" asked the device. I punched "Yes." "No, this is not the correct code number," it scolded. "Try again, please." This time I got it right. "Place your deposit envelope in the Deposit Slot, please," it said, more agreeably, and began to beep slowly.

Now, my wife Cathy usually did this; I couldn't for the life of me figure out where to write my checking account number on the envelope. The machine began to beep more rapidly. The lady waiting behind me cleared her throat several times. "Do you need more time?" the impatient contraption inquired. Flustered, I punched "Yes." The lady mumbled, "Oh, no." Some long minutes later, I gave up. I punched "Cancel transaction" rather forcefully. "Have a nice day," read the sarcastic screen.

Sound familiar? So often our efforts at communicating seem mechanical, unreal, and unsuccessful, don't they? We are the people of the furious pace and the full agenda, so we have learned to be content with minimal exchanges of pleasant words and necessary facts. We fall into the trap of automatic responses, like the woman I know who sat down by a friend and asked, "How are you?" "Not too well," was the reply. "I just got back from a family funeral." And without thinking the woman heard herself answer automatically, "That's nice."

One psychologist found the average amount of significant conversation between the husbands and wives he studied to be 17 minutes a week! That works out to less than 0.2% of their lives. Sometimes we wake up to the startling discovery that many of our most important relationships are suffering from verbal malnutrition.

Jesus had a remarkable way of getting beneath the surface with people, of cutting through the small stuff to get to real, authentic conversation. And he apparently did so without prying or making the other person feel uncomfortable. If we pay close attention, we can learn from him how to get beneath the level of "news, weather, and sports" in our conversations. That's what this chapter is about.

## Levels of Communication

In his fine book *Why Am I Afraid to Tell You Who I Am?*[1], John Powell suggests that when we communicate, we do so at certain levels of openness and self-disclosure:

*Level Five—Cliché Conversation.* This is the safest and most superficial level of communication, little more than a "warm-up" exercise for real conversation. Here the words and subjects are very predictable. "Hello, how are you?" "Just fine, thanks. And you?" "Fine." "What's new with you?" "Nothing much." And so on.

*Level Four—Reporting Facts About Others.* Conversation is more interesting at this, the "news, weather, and sports" level. Here I may gossip. But I do not risk self-disclosure. "I noticed that the Smiths got new carpeting." "Yes, and that reminds me, have you seen Bob's new toupee?"

*Level Three—My Ideas and Judgments.* Here real communication begins. No longer playing it safe, I venture out to display my thinking for the consideration of others. I now become vulnerable to criticism or rejection of my opinions. "I think the mayor's doing a fine job, and here's why . . . " "Here's my theory on that . . . "

*Level Two—My Feelings or Emotions.* At this level I show others not only my head but my heart as well. At what has been called the "gut level," I disclose what is most important to me by communicating what moves me. Here I reveal heartfelt spiritual convictions. "I've never felt happier than when . . . " "I was furious when . . . " "My faith is real to me because . . . "

*Level One—Peak Communication.* This is a very special and mature level of sharing myself with others. Here I am most honest, most open, most vulnerable. Here marriage partners and best friends become trusted listeners with whom the deepest joys, fears, and struggles that need expression can be shared. "I have this sin in my life . . . " "My greatest dream is . . . "

## Beyond Our Fears

Why do we find it so difficult to communicate at those deeper levels, where our real selves can be revealed and expressed? Most likely, because we are afraid. I once read the results of a survey that listed the things and situations that people feared most, and number one on the list was speaking before a group. Ahead of heights, bugs, and deep water!

When I was teaching public speaking courses, I would often see an otherwise bright, confident university student turn into silly putty before my eyes as he stood before the class to give a simple five-minute speech. Stage fright is something we all experience at some time. Mahatma Gandhi may have changed the course of world affairs, but the first time he stood up as a young lawyer to address an Indian court, he became so unnerved that he stood there speechless and finally sat down, having said nothing.

The same fears that grip us in public speaking tend to be the same ones that inhibit healthy communication in our relationships with others. We fear being misunderstood. We fear looking foolish. Most of all, we fear being rejected. John Powell expressed the fear this way: "I am afraid to tell you who I am, because, if I tell you who I am, you may not like who I am, and it's all that I have."

When we begin to understand the fears and insecurities that discourage us from being more open and honest with others, we may also begin to appreciate the good news of a faithful God who promises "Never will I leave you; never will I forsake you" (Heb. 13:5). You see, I can tell you who I am with much greater confidence and transparency once I am convinced that I am securely anchored within the acceptance of God. Your rejection may disappoint me, but it will not devastate me. I care what you think of me, but my self-worth is ultimately measured by the unfailing "steadfast love of the Lord" (Lam. 3:22). "So we say with confidence, 'The Lord is my helper; I will not be afraid. What can man do to me?' " (Heb. 13:6).

## Daring to Be Vulnerable

We will never experience the soul-stirring joys of honest, in-depth conversation until we are willing to make ourselves *vulnerable* to others. What is vulnerability? It means making one's self open or exposed to possible injury; in a word, "woundable." It means dropping your protective barriers, as when "Star Trek's" spaceship *Enterprise* lowers its power shields. Another term for vulnerability is "self-disclosure"—an attempt to put aside masks and hiddenness, and disclose to others "who I am."

The apostle Paul makes himself most vulnerable in his correspondence to, of all churches, the immature Corinthians. He exposes to them his weakness, fear, and trembling (1 Cor. 2:1-4); his distress, anguish, and tears (2 Cor. 2:4); and his painful struggle with his "thorn in the flesh" (2 Cor. 12:7-10). Had you or I been in his place, we might have approached this weak collection of saints with a show of apostolic might and authority. But he amazingly chooses to share with them *his* weaknesses, and invites them to respond in the same spirit: "We have spoken freely to you, Corinthians, and opened wide our hearts to you . . . open wide your hearts also" (2 Cor. 6:11,13). He takes the first step, then invites them to respond in the same spirit.

Since vulnerability is by definition an openness to injury, opening our hearts to others in conversation has its risks. When we drop our shields before others, they may misunderstand us or judge us harshly or exploit us or withdraw from us. But love always carries with it an element of risk. C. S. Lewis has written that to love is to be vulnerable, and the only sure way to make sure your heart will never be bruised or broken by love is never to give it to anyone. "The only place outside Heaven where you can be perfectly safe from all the dangers . . . of love is Hell."[2]

## The Ultimate Vulnerability

The ultimate vulnerability was the incarnation of God in Christ. Think of it. The Creator rubbing elbows with his creatures! "The Word became flesh, and lived for awhile among us." And as a human, the Word made himself woundable, subjecting himself to every human response, including insult, rejection, opposition, and finally, execution. Because Christ did not consider equality with God something to be clutched tightly, he was willing to empty himself of heavenly glory and become a humble servant (Phil. 2:5-8). What if Christ had not been willing to be woundable? Then salvation would not have been possible for you and me, for it is "by his wounds we are healed" (Isa. 53:5).

We should not be surprised, then, when we see Jesus communicating a special kind of openness to others in his words and actions. People did not take up their crosses and follow him because he was merely charismatic and interesting, but because he was compassionate and interested—in them, personally, intimately. The very transparency of his love for others drew them to him.

In conversations with others, Jesus almost immediately found a way of telling them, "You're someone I'd like to get to know." "I'd like a dinner invitation," he told Zacchaeus (Luke

19:5). "You impress me as a man of integrity," he told Nathanael (John 1:47). "I have a nickname for you: 'Peter—the Rock,' " he told Simon (Matt. 16:18). Aren't you drawn to someone who shows that kind of sincere personal interest in you?

When God made himself human to communicate his good news, he opened the channels of communication with his vulnerability. He wept. He rejoiced at weddings. He bounced babies on his knee. He touched us and let us touch him. People will begin to allow us into their lives and conversations at deeper levels—including opportunities to share our faith—when they begin to see that kind of transparent love in us. In the words of an old adage, "They don't care what I know till they know that I care."

## A Conversation at a Well

As we continue to look at how Jesus got beneath the surface with people, let's examine a particular one-to-one encounter. One of the longest recorded conversations in the New Testament is found in John 4, where Jesus talks at length with a Samaritan woman at Jacob's Well. What in this text do we see Jesus doing to move the communication beyond the superficial level?

1. *He noticed her.* Is this too obvious to mention? We often squelch the possibility of good communication by not even seeing the people around us. Can you imagine how many times that woman had made that long, boring trip to get water? Now, for once, someone acknowledged her existence, and a communication channel was opened. Jesus *saw* people.

2. *He prized her uniqueness.* "Let's see, anyone here worth talking to? Just another woman drawing water. Obviously a Samaritan and an immoral one at that (4:18). Nope, nobody here." But Jesus, thank God, did not think that way. He did not allow her categories (woman, Samaritan, sinner) to prejudice him against her. He saw a uniquely precious lady and refused to reject her categorically. Jesus *accepted* people.

3. *He asked for her help.* Jesus broke the ice with, "Will you give me a drink?" Most people respond very positively to a

**66**

*Sometimes we wake up
to the startling discovery
that many of our most important
relationships are suffering
from verbal malnutrition.*

**99**

simple request for assistance. Even in New York City I have never failed to get help with directions when I needed it, if I stood long enough and looked bewildered enough. It makes others feel good to know they have rendered a service. Jesus let people *serve* him.

4. *He talked about what was important to her.* Water. That's what brought her to this place—a basic human need. Jesus used as a point of contact a subject he knew might interest her. He did not insist that she come to his area of interest; he came to hers. Where can you get this living water?" she asked eagerly (4:11). Jesus showed *interest* in people's needs.

5. *He kept the conversation on track.* Notice how the woman tried to divert the conversation onto safe doctrinal ground when it began to touch on personal matters like her marital situation. "What about the true mountain of worship?" she asked evasively (4:20). "No," Jesus countered, "let's talk about how we can be true worshipers" (See 4:23-24). Jesus kept conversations at a significant *personal level.*

6. *He revealed his identity.* Having earned her trust with his acceptance and interest, Jesus was then able to reveal himself fully to the woman: "I who speak to you am the Messiah" (4:26). He took a risk. She could have laughed or spat or walked away, but she believed. Jesus knew how and when to *disclose himself* to others.

This was a conversation that never should have taken place, according to the social norms of the day. But because Jesus initiated it and pushed it beyond superficialities, a woman's life was redirected, and a doorway to faith was opened to an entire town (4:39-42).

## The Human Touch

Many important messages (particularly religious messages) are never received because, while the content is factual, the delivery lacks the human touch. A check-out girl says in a tired and unconvincing tone, "Thank you for shopping at our store. Have a nice day." A computerized letter begins, "Dear friend . . . " A sign by the highway reads, "Jesus saves." Or a bumper sticker instructs, "Smile, God loves you." What is lacking? The human touch. The warmth and depth that a message has when it is delivered in an obviously caring way.

There is no substitute for the human touch when it comes to deepening communication, whether it is an actual hug or handshake, or simply a smile or look of keen interest. Did you know that people can die from lack of human contact? Just such a disease exists; it is called *marasmus* (meaning "wasting away") and usually afflicts the very young and the very old. We need more than just words from others; we also need nonverbal signals that they care.

Jesus of Nazareth was one of the most powerful *nonverbal* communicators ever. His words cut through people's pretenses and masks, to be sure, but it was his real, human touch that made those words powerfully credible.

A leper came to Jesus. The leper is history's most familiar "untouchable." So someone in the crowd probably gasped when Jesus reached out and *touched* the diseased man and made him whole (Mark 1: 40-42). Jesus' touch may not have been necessary for the leper's physical healing, but it probably was critical for his emotional healing. For Jesus knew that sometimes a man with a diseased body can have a diseased self-image as well.[3] So when he healed, he almost always touched—blind eyes, deaf ears, mute tongues.

When Gandhi moved among the people of India, they would try to touch him, believing his mere touch could bring them a healing or a blessing. Often he had to have his feet and legs massaged with ointment, because they were so sore and bruised from the people's touch. Jesus got the same treatment from the crowds of his day (Luke 8:42-48). Doubtless, our Lord spent many evenings tending to the bruises he had earned by being touchable. Jesus had the right touch—not affected, not sensual, but a gentle, caring touch that reassured others of his genuine interest. No wonder they opened their hearts to him.

## Getting Beneath the Surface

If we are serious about getting beyond the small talk of news, weather, and sports with others, here are some practical suggestions:

• Encourage others to talk about their interests, opinions, and feelings. Learn to be an encouraging listener. Develop and demonstrate a deeper interest in others.

• Learn people's names when you first meet them. My name is an important part of who I am. Others are flattered when we make the effort to remember.

• When you encounter defensiveness in others, do not attack it: "What's the matter, are you afraid to be open and honest?" or "Oh, get real for a change!"

• Create opportunities for unpressured conversation in comfortable settings. Let people know you want to be with them. "How about a cup of coffee?" "Let's go for a walk."

• Always keep a confidence. Respect others' vulnerability when they open up to you. Nothing discourages vulnerability like gossip.

• Don't be argumentative. When others start revealing their personal opinions and feelings, you won't always agree. You can state differing views without trying to win the conversation.

• You cannot force self-disclosure on others. Many people are not ready for immediate vulnerability and will retreat quickly. As you attempt to move into deeper levels of communication, go slowly and sensitively.

• Admit to others your faults, needs, and fears. Some Christians think it's unspiritual to admit any weakness or struggle. But genuinely transparent persons (like David, Jeremiah, Paul, and Jesus) have always been more attractive and credible than those who wear masks of religious perfectionism.

The English statesman, Oliver Cromwell, once sat for a portrait by the court painter. When he discovered that the painter had failed to include the many warts on his face in the picture, Cromwell insisted, "Paint me warts and all!" Secure in the

steadfast love and acceptance of God, we can dare to be ourselves with others, warts and all. Only then will we begin to
experience the profound joys of honest, in-depth communication.

[1]John Powell, *Why Am I Afraid to Tell You Who I Am?* (Allen, TX: Argus
Communications, 1969), pp. 50-62.
[2]C. S. Lewis, *The Four Loves* (New York: Harcourt Brace Jovanovich,
1960), p. 169.
[3]Rebecca Manley Pippert, *Out of the Saltshaker & Into the World* (Downers
Grove, IL: IVP, 1979), p. 38.

# 8

# *Is Anybody Listening?*

Reuben Welch recalls this picture from his childhood in rural California: Often people would drive the twenty miles from the nearest town just to talk to his father, a quiet man. As the visitor would pour out problems and emotions, he could hear his father responding with comments like, "Hm-m . . . my, my . . . Well, what do you know . . . Hmph, yes sir." After a while, the visitor would thank Welch's father and return to town. Looking back on those exchanges, Welch reflected, "Twenty miles is not too far to go to talk to someone who will listen and care and look and understand and hear, even if all he says is, "Well, what do you know.' "[1]

Deep within every human being is a yearning to be heard. We all have a story to tell: *our* story, our unique life perspective and experience. Thomas Hart puts it well: "There is nothing quite so sacred, so fragile, or so mysterious as a human being. There is probably no service we can render other persons quite as great or important as to be listener and receiver to them in those moments when they need to open their hearts and tell someone their story."[2]

James surely had that yearning need in mind when he

97

counseled Christians to "be quick to listen, slow to speak" (James 1:19).

But who is listening? Many people have yet to find that "quick listener," one who is ready and eager to give them a hearing. Rather, they have encountered only an endless succession of indifferent listeners and quick talkers. Today's course offerings and textbooks on communication point to a dramatic imbalance between speaking skills and listening skills. They deal almost exclusively with *output*—how to be an effective public speaker or conversationalist. In contrast, little attention is given to the question of *intake*—how to receive the information others want to communicate. Many are being trained to speak well but few to listen well. Having too many talkers and too few listeners creates a serious communication imbalance, resulting in what Dr. Paul Tournier called "dialogues of the deaf."

## LEARNING THE SKILL OF CHRISTIAN LISTENING

A well-known preacher came to visit in our home. We, along with thousands of others, had long appreciated this man's ability to communicate Christian ideas. But as we sat around our living room with him, something became quickly apparent about his communication skills at a conversational level: he was a lousy listener! He dominated the conversation, treating our remarks pretty much as interruptions in his flow of thought. He never invited my wife Cathy's participation in the discussion, never even looked at her while he was talking. He was an articulate, intelligent, entertaining guest. But he did not pay us the courtesy of listening.

Many of us preachers and other public speakers are guilty of being too geared to output and not enough to intake. So I admire (and even envy a bit) the truly good listeners I know. Most of them will tell you that, for them, listening well is not a natural ability but a learned skill. As with any fine skill, learning how to listen requires effort and determination.

If we honestly desire to be more useful to others and to God, we must submit to the discipline required in becoming "quick to listen." Then we'll find ourselves maturing in several key areas—understanding one another, working hard for one another, participating actively as we listen, growing in Christ, and becoming more like him. Let's look at each area individually.

## To Listen, to Understand

What is Christian listening? It is attention with the intention to understand another person. Christian listening is an act which communicates to another, "Right now, I am here for *you*. No one else, just you. I want to hear and understand what you have to say. I'm all yours." Listening is allowing the other person to set the agenda for the conversation, seeking to clarify his point of view. Ultimately, listening is helping a person to understand himself better. As Benjamin Disraeli said, "The greatest good you can do for another is not just to share your riches but to reveal to him his own."

Helping a hurting person to verbalize his struggles has tremendous therapeutic value. Sometimes a person will come to me for counseling and say as we begin, "Now I don't expect you to have any answers for me." My internal response to that is, "Thanks for the vote of confidence!" But in fact their expectation is healthy. Some of the best answers will be the ones they discover within themselves—answers to questions such as, "What am I feeling and why?" and "What can I do about it?"

What is true of the human body is likewise true of the human spirit—people have considerable internal resources for getting better. You do not have to be a trained analyst to be a resourceful listener. The healing attentions of empathy and friendship are often more valuable than words of wisdom. It is amazing how light can break through and how pain can dissipate in the presence of a caring, supportive Christian listener.

But listening can be counterfeited: maintaining a polite silence while the other person speaks, all the while mentally rehearsing one's own insights and opinions, to be inserted at the earliest possible opening. In his beautiful "Hillside Prayer,"

Francis of Assisi prayed, "Lord, grant that I may seek more to understand than to be understood." Do you want to "lay down your life for your brother" (1 John 3:16) in a concrete, practical way? Give him your exclusive interest and undivided attention when he needs to be heard. Give him yourself.

## To Listen, to Work Hard

Being a good listener is hard work, but it is a labor of Christian love. We must be willing to commit significant blocks of time to others. One who is hurting or confused, may not tell his story in a clear, organized, straightforward fashion. Listening to such a person requires concentration and strenuous mental effort.

We can listen five times as fast as we can speak; that is, you may be speaking at 100 words a minute, but I can listen to you at up to 500 words a minute. The brain can process thoughts far more rapidly than we can speak. So we all have to fight the "wandering mind" temptation, particularly in a lengthy conversation.[3] Sometimes we have to work harder to listen well than we do to speak well.

Committing yourself to be a caring listener means committing yourself to personal inconvenience and discomfort. "Carry each other's burdens" was not intended to be a sweet-sounding religious sentiment; God clearly calls us to burden ourselves with the loads others are shouldering. No, it is not pleasant being another person's dumpsite—letting them unload on us their guilt, pain, hostility, and frustration. Most of us agree with Lucy in "Peanuts," when she said, "I don't want ups and downs. I want ups and ups and ups!" Committing to listen will expose us to sadness, ugliness, boredom, imposition, and even manipulation. Listening is costly. Christian discipleship is costly. But it is in the bearing of our mutual burdens, Paul said, that we "fulfill the law of Christ" (Gal. 6:2).

Some people seem to have more natural aptitude as listeners than others. But there are certain listening skills that all of us can improve with practice. Each Christian is, after all, a "servant

**66**

Deep within every
human being is a yearning
to be heard. We all have a story to
tell: our story, our unique life
perspective and experience.

**99**

in training," steadily growing in maturity toward the perfect standard of Christ (Eph. 4:12-13). As we learn to listen more attentively, we grow in our capacity to do something Jesus did consistently in his earthly ministry: take people seriously. Becoming an effective listener calls for as much discipline and practice as becoming an effective speaker. And as always, there is much to be learned about how to treat people by fixing our eyes on Jesus.

## To Listen, to Become Involved

Proverbs 20:5 says, "The purposes of a man's heart are deep waters, but a man of understanding draws them out." A passive listener, one who sits in blank-faced silence, is little better than no listener at all. But if we are serious about growing as listeners and aspire to be "men/women of understanding," we must do more than sit and stare.

How do we "draw out the deep waters"? Good questions help. Always taking care not to pry or pump for information, we can utilize simple door-openers such as these: "I would like to hear what you think." "Tell me about it." "Go on, I'm listening." "Would you like to talk more about this?" "This seems to be something you feel pretty strongly about."

Once a conversation is underway, we can invite further sharing by using these comments: "I see." "Right." "Uh-huh." "What then?" Simple verbal responses like these (along with nonverbal responses such as nods and smiles) are more important than they may seem. They are signals of acceptance, reassuring the speaker of our continuing interest. In this way, we can communicate without interrupting his flow of thought, "It's okay to keep talking . . . I'm not going anywhere . . . I'm here for you."

An involved listener also aids and encourages the speaker by occasionally repeating his ideas and feelings back to him: "Let me see if I'm hearing you correctly. Are you saying . . . ?" "You're pretty upset about this, aren't you?" "So what you really mean is . . . " Such feedback demonstrates the listener's sincere intention to understand the speaker. And, it gives the speaker a chance to clarify, correct, or amplify his ideas.

## To Listen, to Grow

If it is our life's highest aim to know Christ and to grow in him, we must learn to listen—to God and to one another. In the familiar words from the Old Testament, "Be still and know that I am God" (Ps. 46:10), we can almost hear a loving Father saying, "Hush! Will you please be quiet and listen to me for a moment?" Before the throne of Almighty God, man's only appropriate response is to be a reverential listener: "Guard your steps when you go to the house of God. *Go near to listen* rather than to offer the sacrifice of fools, who do not know that they do wrong. Do not be quick with your mouth, do not be hasty in your heart to utter anything before God. God is in heaven and you are on earth, so let your words be few" (Ecc. 5:1-2).

All who would follow God's Son must develop an attentive ear to God's word. Jesus described himself as a loving shepherd whose sheep know his voice and *listen* to it (John 10:3-4). The Christian's faith, Paul said, "comes from *hearing* the message, and the message is heard through the word of Christ" (Rom. 10:17). The word of God is our sure guide to faith, but we must supply the obedient listening ear. Jesus identified the wise man with the indestructable house as he who "hears these words of mine and puts them into practice" (Matt. 7:24). As Jesus instructs us through the pages of scripture, God prompts us as he did those men at the transfiguration, "This is my Son, whom I love; with him I am well pleased. *Listen to him*" (Matt. 17:5).

God also makes us grow as we listen to the counsel of spiritually mature Christian brothers and sisters. "The way of a fool seems right to him, but a wise man listens to advice" (Prov. 12:15). Christians are to attend to the lives of godly leaders (Heb. 13:7). How tragic it is that older Christians often are a neglected natural resource within the church. A Jewish proverb says, "Listen gladly to every godly argument. . . . If you discover a wise man, rise early to visit him; let your feet wear out his doorstep."

There is yet another growth-by-listening process: We grow as we share life's struggles, failures, and victories. Within the Christian family, we listen as others lay upon us their burdens (Gal. 6:2), confess to us their sins (James 5:16), and share with us their joys and their tears (Rom. 12:15). As we tune in to others, God teaches us profound lessons in compassion, humility, forgiveness, and thankfulness. If we are to experience and encourage authentic growth in Christ, we must be open to God and open to others—attentive, interested, teachable—in short, "quick to listen."

## To Listen, to Be like Jesus

For many of us, the picture of Jesus that first leaps to mind is that the Teacher, the public speaker—speaking simple, powerful beatitudes on the mount or telling a masterful parable in the marketplace. But Jesus was not exclusively a preacher. Far from it. He spent a large part of his ministry in one-to-one conversations. He talked and listened to rabbis and fishermen, publicans and prostitutes, lepers and lawyers, Gentiles and Jews. In those conversations we not only see such key listening qualities as genuineness, compassion, and respect, but we also see him doing three vital things to facilitate better listening:

*He Made Himself Available.* When it was known that Jesus was coming to town, the people gathered and placed the sick in the marketplaces (Mark 6:56). Everyone knew that Jesus would be where the people were. He was no ivory-tower Messiah; had no "by appointment only" policy. He would go to any open synagogue, sit at any man's table. It was his uncommon availability to all sorts of people that earned him harsh criticism and false accusation from the religious community: "Here is a glutton and a drunkard, a friend of tax collectors and sinners" (Matt. 11:19). Jesus consistently sought out the personal contact with others that is essential to keeping communication lines open.

*He Allowed Himself to Be Interrupted.* Have you ever noticed how many of the significant personal encounters in Jesus' life occurred as he was "on the way" to something else? He was on the way to attend to Jairus' daughter when he healed the woman with the hemorrhage (Mark 5:24-34). He was on his way to Jerusalem when the rich young ruler interrupted his journey (Mark 10:17). Jesus used his time carefully; he had much to do in a brief three-year ministry. But his schedule was flexible and interruptable, because he was "a man for others." We can have few opportunities to perform the service of listening, if we so tightly schedule our lives that others always get a busy signal from us.

*He Asked Good Questions.* Jesus often encouraged others to open their hearts to him by the use of simple, direct questions. He asked questions such as these to his disciples: "What about you? Who do you say I am?" (Matt. 16:15); to two men on the road to Emmaus: "What are you discussing together as you walk along?" (Luke 24:17); to an invalid: "Do you want to get well?" (John 5:6); to a man born blind: "Do you believe in the Son of Man?" (John 9:35); to Peter: "Simon, son of John, do you truly love me?" (John 21:16). With such questions he opened doors for conversation and invited others in. Many people never share anything from the heart until they first receive what they perceive to be a sincere invitation to do so.

## HOW TO BE A BETTER LISTENER

*Evaluate Yourself as a Listener.* Many Christians have never taken stock of their ability to tune in to others and thus may never have made a conscious effort to improve their listening skills. Try asking a trusted friend, "Do you find me to be a good listener?" Then brace yourself for the answer! (This is especially recommended for husbands and wives.) Engage in some honest self-examination by looking for signs of poor listening habits: Your mind often wanders while others are speaking; you can't remember important details from conversations; you find yourself misquoting others frequently; you easily get impatient when someone else is talking; you interrupt a lot; or, you often find yourself "filibustering"—dominating conversations so you won't

have to listen to others. Apply the Golden Rule principle to your
listening: Listen to others as you would have them listen to you.

*Minimize the Distractions.* Undivided attention is usually the
most appreciated attention. A standard cartoon gag shows a
husband and wife at breakfast, he behind the morning paper and
she laboring in vain to communicate with him. When Jesus
wanted to have a good talk with his Father, he deliberately
sought out quiet times (Mark 1:35) and quiet places (Luke 5:16).
We too must seek out times and places that minimize distractions
and maximize good conversation. Once I attempted to lead an
evangelistic Bible study in a men's dormitory room with a cover
girl poster on the wall just above and behind me. That setting
was definitely not conducive to good listening! To say, "Why
don't we go somewhere where we can talk more freely," or,
"Give me a few minutes to finish what I'm into here, then I can
give you my undivided attention," indicates how serious you are
about your listening.

*Meet the Speaker's Eyes.* As Jesus was speaking with the rich
young ruler, Mark records that "Jesus looked at him and loved
him" (10:21). It is apparent that Jesus looked intently at the
young man and saw in his face and eyes qualities that moved
him deeply. Look at the person as you listen to him. In so doing
you will communicate your attentiveness to his needs, focus
your own attention, and pick up valuable nonverbal cues such
as facial expressions, nervous movements, or tears. Good eye
contact requires concentration and practice; many find it difficult
and uncomfortable to maintain for more than a few seconds at a
time. But speech studies have found that regular eye contact
enhances and encourages better communication. Don't "dim
your lights." Look people directly in the eyes as they speak; they
will be flattered and reassured by indications of loving interest.

*Maintain Your Christian Integrity.* Listening is not a game
but a profound trust. When a person entrusts his story to you
and draws back the curtain of his life, you must respect
and protect that disclosure with the greatest possible care. A
Christian listener must never violate a confidence by gossiping

(Prov. 11:13). Spread personal information shared with you, and watch the doors into others' lives slam shut to you. Also, never make listening into an artificial or affected technique. With the availability of so many paperback personality-repair manuals today, anyone can become an amateur psychologist. But Jesus did not approach people with artificial techniques. Every person was special to him, and when he conversed with them, they felt special. Jesus treated people right; so must we.

*Be Quick to Listen, Slow to Speak.* A biblical proverb says, "He who answers before listening—that is his folly and shame" (Prov. 18:13). In fact, at least sixteen of the proverbs are warnings about people who talk too much! (See also Prov. 10:19, 13:3, 15:28, 29:20.) Being "quick to listen, slow to speak" means hearing the other person out, not interrupting, and not attempting to fill every verbal vacuum with your comments. Many of us feel uncomfortable with a moment of silence in a conversation; we want to "fill in the blank." Or, we feel we need to provide the other person with an answer as quickly as possible. Instead of really listening, we busy ourselves mentally formulating a good response.

So let's shut up and work on our listening, shall we? Put down the paper, Dad. Lay aside the magazine, Mom. Turn off the television, America! If Christians are to be men and women whose lives are distinctively for others as our Lord's life clearly was, one of the very best ways of demonstrating to others that we are "for" them is to listen to them. Apply the old formula, "Stop—Look—Listen." When someone needs to tell his story, whatever else you are doing, look him squarely in the eye, and listen as you believe Jesus would.

[1] Reuben Welch, *We Really Do Need Each Other* (Nashville: Impact Books, 1973), pp. 103-104. Used by permission of Zondervan Publishing House

[2] Thomas N. Hart, *The Art of Christian Listening* (New York: Paulist Press, 1980), p. 1.

[3] H. Norman Wright, *Training Christians to Counsel* (Denver: Christian Marriage Enrichment, 1977), p. 30.

# 9

# *When We Don't Agree*

I sit in the living room of a couple who have been married thirty-five years, listening to them scream at one another through me. If they ever could communicate with each other, they've forgotten how. They apparently quit listening to each other years ago. Now neither will budge an inch in the other's direction. So they pour out all their accusations, insults, and anger for the other through a third party. They remind me of the two first-down markers at a football game: chained together but always ten yards apart.

A woman tells about her mother's novel way of communicating her grievances and disapproval to the family: She voices her complaints to the family dog (for everyone's else's benefit). "Well, Buster, that was a fine way for them to treat me! I'd be ashamed of myself if I'd acted that way, wouldn't you?"

Two young people come for marriage counseling. They've only been married a year, but already a conflict pattern has been firmly established and is repeating itself with terrible predictability: They disagree. She loses her temper and yells at him. He grows silent. She yells louder. He withdraws. She cries. He walks away.

Conflict—it's inevitable in a world where every individual

is unique and, therefore, different from every other individual. We look at the world differently, you and I. My needs, my ideas, my interests, my vocabulary, and my style are not the same as yours. And the longer and deeper you and I communicate, the more those differences will come up.

Conflict means "to strike together; a fight, battle, struggle; sharp disagreement or collision in interests or ideas." Conflict, like anger, is not in and of itself a sin. The spiritual issue is, how do we respond to conflicts? How do we speak and behave in a conflict situation? Do we work toward resolution, or do we expect the other person to do all the work? Do we respond to conflict with words of reconciliation or words of retaliation?

## Where Conflict Begins

James is one of the bluntest and most straightforward writers in scripture. In James 4, he gives us an incisive analysis of the origins and motives of destructive conflict:

"What causes fights and quarrels among you? Don't they come from your desires that battle within you? You want something but don't get it. You kill and covet, but you cannot have what you want. You quarrel and fight. You do not have, because you do not ask God. When you ask, you do not receive, because you ask with wrong motives, that you may spend what you get on your pleasures" (Jas. 4:1-3).

Why do we fume and fuss? Whether the conflict is between two individuals, two families, or two nations, it usually boils down to this: "I want my way, and I'll do whatever it takes to get my way."

Our "desires" (4:1) often cause us to fire the first shot in the war of conflict, James says. The word *hēdonōn* in Greek, which literally means "pleasures," giving us our English word "hedonistic." Hedonism is life according to the pleasure principle: I will do as I *please*. James contends that it is this hedonistic spirit that turns mere differences into open warfare.

Between marriage partners, the most trivial of differences have been known to touch off bloody verbal warfare. He prefers the electric blanket on a toasty "High" setting; she sleeps best on "Low" (What did we do before dual controls?) He likes the toilet paper to loop over in the dispenser; she feels strongly that it should turn under. He likes his tomato soup made with milk; her mother always made it with water.

The initial issue may be silly and insignificant. If you laugh at it and work out an agreement, the emotions quickly blow over. But if even trivial issues are left unresolved, they can become magnified into a much more volatile issue: Your way versus my way. Who will have their desires satisfied? Who will win this battle?

The ancient story of Naboth's vineyard (1 Kings 21) provides a classic and deadly example of James' conflict pattern in real life. King Ahab wanted Naboth's vineyard. Naboth refused. Ahab pouted. Queen Jezebel, a resourceful lady, conspired to engineer Naboth's death. And Ahab got the vineyard he wanted. "Then, after desire has conceived, it gives birth to sin; and sin, when it is full-grown, gives birth to death" (Jas. 1:15).

## Why We Disagree

One of Teddy Roosevelt's sons once said of him, "Father always wants to be the bride at every wedding and the corpse at every funeral." At times we all operate on the assumption that the universe revolves around us, don't we? Our human tendency to place our needs at the center of every issue invariably leads us into conflict.

The first shot that touches off the hurtful wars of conflict, James teaches us, is invariably selfish human desire: I want what I want. It is not accidental that the great foundation of Judeo-Christian ethics, the Ten Commandments, conclude with the imperative, "You shall not covet" (Ex. 20:17). Whenever we enter conflict with the spirit of covetousness or hedonistic desire, disaster awaits us, for we have adopted an anti-God state of mind. Covetousness, or greed, is nothing less than idolatry (Col. 3:5). I don't want what God can give me (Jas. 4:2); I'm not interested in God's way or your way; I want it my way.

But let's not forget, not all conflict is the result of selfishness and covetousness. Sometimes we will disagree simply because we are different. Even in the oneness of marriage, partners should not expect to become clones of one another. Marriage can be likened to two clay figures, both with uniquely distinctive characteristics. If the two figures are pressed together, side by side, and then baked in a kiln, they will become one figure. But they will still retain their individual distinctiveness. "The two shall become one flesh. So they are no longer two, but one" (Matt. 19:5-6). But they are still different persons. And those differences will at times produce conflict.

## RESOLVING TO RESOLVE OUR CONFLICTS

One cold winter's day a few years ago, I came upon a woman trying to get her car off an icy spot in a drugstore parking lot. Her rear tires were just spinning in place. One fellow was already behind her car and started pushing. I joined him, and we pushed, but the car went nowhere. Within minutes, six of us were pushing that car, and still nothing was happening. Finally someone thought to ask, "Lady, is your emergency brake on?" Sheepishly she released her brake and drove away.

Finding yourself locked into a repeating conflict cycle is like trying to move forward with the emergency brake on—lots of commotion, but no motion. Others can advise us, encourage us, push us, but until we release the brakes we'll get nowhere. The brakes might be our pride or fear or anger or just poor habits of resolving conflict.

Conflict resolution is seldom easy. But it is the way of Christ, a prime way we show that the love of Christ dwells richly in us. When reports got back to Paul that believers in Corinth were dragging other believers into the local courts to settle their disputes before pagan judges, the apostle was exasperated. "Shame on you!" he wrote back. "Couldn't you work this out among yourselves?" (See 1 Cor. 6:1-8). In Christ, we have all the teaching, examples, motivation, and power we need to work toward resolution of our conflicts, especially with other Christians.

With God's help, we can find the resolve we need to resolve our conflicts. Here are four fundamental resolutions we'll need to make:

- I resolve not to be quarrelsome.
- I resolve to accept responsibility for my role in our problem.
- I resolve to accept you as you are.
- I resolve to forgive you.

## I Resolve Not to Be Quarrelsome

"As charcoal to embers and as wood to fire, so is a quarrelsome man for kindling strife" (Prov. 26:21). While some conflict is inevitable and even productive in relationships, quarrelsomeness—continued verbal hostility—is never productive. It can drain a relationship dry of cooperation, productivity, and joy.

The ancient sages of Israel had nothing but scorn for the person who constantly bickers and argues: "He who loves a quarrel loves sin" (Prov. 17:19). "It is to a man's honor to avoid strife, but every fool is quick to quarrel" (Prov. 20:3). "A quarrelsome wife is like a constant dripping on a rainy day" (Prov. 27:15). I know of a man who complains to his wife about her cooking at dinner time every night; not just once in a while when the food's lukewarm or unsalted, but every night. Husbands can be pretty drippy, too.

Quarreling is the verbal process of resolution stuck in neutral. The grievances are being laid on the table, but nothing constructive is being done with them. Sometimes quarreling is just a long-established pattern of insensitivity. But sometimes it's a grueling and unproductive attempt at conflict resolution: Like the infamous Chinese water torture, I direct a steady, nagging drip-drip-drip of complaint against your defenses in hopes that you'll give in. But will my nagging help bring us to a peaceable resolution? Hardly ever. More likely, you'll either give in to me resentfully or continue to resist me resentfully.

Quarrelsomeness is a fire of irritability that functions like a pilot light, always burning, ready at any moment to touch off a major combustion. Pride is again the chief villain. I want things my way. "Pride only breeds quarrels, but wisdom is found in those who take advice" (Prov. 13:10). Until we resolve to let God help us conquer our pride and move beyond the quarreling stage of conflict, we'll just continue to spin our wheels in painful frustration.

### I Resolve to Accept My Responsibility

It's just plain hard to say, "I was wrong." I believe some folks might sprain every muscle in their mouths were they ever to allow their lips to formulate those never-before-mentioned words! Do we feel like it's weak and undignified to confess our wrongs? Elton Trueblood corrects that kind of wrong-headed thinking: "Seldom in a man's life is he actually nobler than when he says, 'I was wrong; I am ashamed; please forgive me.' " *(The Lord's Prayers).*

If we are to find our way to resolution, here's my first assignment: I must accept *my share* of responsibility for the conflict, not erect my defenses and try to pin all the blame on you. What have *I* done to contribute to our problem? And what am *I* doing to facilitate its resolution?

Then, when we talk about the conflict, I can sincerely send you what have been called "I-messages." An "I-message" communicates my acceptance of responsibility: "Our relationship is very important to me, and right now I'm feeling some conflict between us. As I see it, our problem is _____, and I've contributed to the problem by _____. Please forgive me. I'd really like to hear your side of this; can we talk about it?"[1]

On the other hand, a "you-message" puts the burden of the conflict on the other person and virtually assures that nothing will get resolved: "Well, you did it again! Things were going along just fine until you _____. You don't care about anybody but yourself. You make me so mad!" Instead of attacking the problem, we attack the other person. A "you-message" says, "Things are really messed up between us, and it's *all your fault.*"

James 5:16 has powerful implications for conflict resolution: "Confess your sins to each other and pray for the other." If I love you more than I love a victory over you, I should be able to swallow my pride and accept my share of the responsibility for our conflict.

## I Resolve to Accept You

An old show tune captures some of the frustration of coming to terms with a person different from ourselves: "You say 'potato' and I say 'po-tah-to,' you say 'tomato' and I say 'to-mah-to,' . . . Let's call the whole thing off!"

Accepting the other person as different from ourselves is one of the most difficult and indispensable aspects of conflict resolution. "Why can't they see it my way?" we wonder. Because they see it *their* way, that's why.

In Romans 14-15, Paul exhorts a diverse Christian community in Rome to bear with one another's differences in lifestyle and religious upbringing. "Accept one another, then," he says, "just as Christ accepted you, in order to bring praise to God" (Rom. 15:7). Yes, the Bible teaches elsewhere that some doctrines and lifestyles are unacceptable among believers. But Paul's argument here is, Christ accepted us, fallible and weak as we are, into his family. He didn't give up on us at the first sign of weakness or individuality. We must extend the same grace to one another and learn to accept one another in spite of racial, regional, or stylistic differences.

When I do premarriage counseling with a couple, I always have them take a test which measures certain individual personality variables and tendencies—such as, do they tend to be nervous or composed, inhibited or expressive, impulsive or self-disciplined. The main value of the test is to help them see their similarities and differences. It isn't essential that a couple be carbon copies of one other to have a healthy marriage; it *is* essential that they see and accept one another as they truly are.

### I Resolve to Forgive You

A teenager asked a minister for counsel. "I left home and did something that'll make my dad furious with me when he finds out. What should I do?" The minister replied, "Go home and confess your sin to him, and he'll probably forgive you and treat you like the prodigal son." Sometime later the boy reported to the minister, "Well, I told Dad what I did." "And did he kill the fatted calf for you?" asked the minister. "No," said the boy, "but he nearly killed the prodigal son!"

A forgiving spirit will open the doors to conflict resolution; an unforgiving spirit will keep them closed. No story in the scriptures pictures God's willingness to restore relationship with us more warmly than the Prodigal Son (Luke 15:11-27). But Jesus was quite outspoken on this point—the forgiven people must be willing to forgive.

When it comes to conflicts between his followers, Jesus' teaching can be summed up pretty simply: Work it out right away, because an obstacle between two of you is also an obstacle between each of you and the Father. "So when you offer your gift to God at the altar, and you remember that your brother has something against you, leave your gift there at the altar. Go and make peace with him. Then come and offer your gift" (Matt. 5:23-24, New Century Version). Obviously Jesus does not consider reconciliation to be an optional extra in our relationships. When we're not looking to make peace with our fellow Christians, then neither are we in the right frame of mind to worship God.

Forgiveness is a prerequisite to all healthy relationships. Writing from a Nazi prison, Dietrich Bonhoeffer challenged a young bride and groom to forgive and to accept one another:

> In a word, live together in forgiveness, for without it
> no human relationship, least of all a marriage, can
> survive. Don't insist on your rights, . . . don't find fault

**66**

*Our human tendency
to place our own needs
at the center of every issue
invariably leads
to conflict.*

**99**

with each other, but accept each other as you are, and forgive each other every day from the bottom of your hearts.[2]

## CONFLICTS IN THE NEW TESTAMENT

By looking to the ministry of Jesus and the life of the early church, we can find some very practical case studies in Christian conflict resolution. The first two cases involve Jesus and his opponents; the next two occur within the Christian community. Notice how differently each of these conflicts was resolved.

### Jesus and the Pharisees (Mark 3:1-6)

**Conflict:** Jewish legal tradition limited, among other activities, the practice of medicine and healing on the Sabbath. Cases of life and death were considered exceptions to the Sabbath law, but a man's shriveled hand did not constitute such an exception.

**Resolution:** Jesus healed the man, contending that "doing good" was as lawful on the Sabbath as "saving life." Notice that Jesus was the one who raised the conflict issue on this occasion; his opponents remained silent. Also notice that he could have compromised by waiting until the next day to heal the man, but in so doing he would have avoided the crucial issue of which was more important to God, man or the Sabbath (Mark 2:27).

### Jesus and the Sanhedrin (John 11:45-54)

**Conflict:** Jesus' popularity and power posed a threat to the religious establishment, so Jewish leaders began to plot his arrest and execution.

**Resolution:** Rather than have his ministry end prematurely, Jesus distanced himself from his enemies for a while. Notice here that when Jesus saw how volatile the conflict situation had become, he chose at this time the strategy of withdrawal. Sometimes simply avoiding conflict resolves it; in this case, however, withdrawal only postponed the ultimate resolution.

**Jewish and Gentile Church Leaders** (Acts 15:1-35)

**Conflict:** Leaders among the predominantly Jewish churches in Judaea were insisting that Gentile converts to Christianity be circumcised according to the law of Moses.

**Resolution:** Apostles, elders, and other church leaders met in Jerusalem to discuss the issue in depth. After hearing reports and recommendations from men such as Paul and James, they worked out a mutually satisfactory resolution: The entire old law, including circumcision, was not to be bound on Gentile Christians; however, the Gentiles were called upon to abstain from practices offensive to their Jewish brothers, such as eating the blood and meat of strangled animals, and sexual immorality. Notice how both sides listened to one another, made sizeable concessions to the other, and set forth their resolution clearly in writing.

**Paul and Barnabas** (Acts 15:36-41)

**Conflict:** Paul refused to take along young Mark as a missionary companion, because Mark had dropped out on a previous journey. Barnabas wanted to take Mark (his cousin) with them, thus prompting a "sharp disagreement" between Barnabas and Paul.

**Resolution:** Paul and Barnabas agreed to disagree and parted company for a time. Paul and Silas headed up to Syria, while Barnabas and Mark set sail for Cyprus. Notice that two mission efforts, instead of one, resulted. It's important to note that Paul and Mark were later reconciled, so much so that Paul describes Mark as one who "is helpful to me in my ministry" (2 Tim. 4:11).

## DEALING WITH CONFLICT

In his book *Caring Enough to Confront*,[3] David Augsburger describes five different ways that people deal with conflict situations. They are summarized as follows:

1. *My Way* (I win). I assert my will until you finally give in. I am totally right and you are totally wrong. My way is the only way.

"My Way" is the covetous, hedonistic option; it shows no concern for your needs, because my needs are all that matter.

2. *No Way* (I withdraw). I bury my feelings and walk away from the conflict. Nothing is resolved, because conflicts are to be avoided at all costs.

"No Way" lacks the aggressive, arrogant spirit but still shows little concern for your needs.

3. *Your Way* (I give in). I yield to you because I do not want to lose your approval. I will maintain a submissive position no matter what frustrations I feel inside.

"Your Way" may appear outwardly to be a "nicer" style but can be at heart dishonest and cowardly.

4. *Half Way* (We compromise). I win some and lose some, give a little to gain a little, as do you. My half of the truth added to your half may result in agreement, but it may not give us the whole truth or the best resolution to our conflict.

"Half Way" beats the first three options in its concern to strike a compromise that benefits both sides; however, there is a better model for resolution that "Let's Make a Deal."

5. *Our Way* (We work out mutual goals). Because I care about our relationship, I am committed to working towards a resolution that will neither sacrifice your integrity and goals, nor mine. As we resolve conflict, we discover new mutual goals and possibilities.

"Our Way" is the high road, the strongest option, the selfless approach. It could be called "Christ's Way." Everyone we come into conflict with will not share or choose to live by kingdom values, it's true. But there is no limit to the healing that can come to our relationships when we approach conflict looking "not only to our own interests, but also to the interests of others" (Phil. 2:4).

## Communication Rules for Resolution

The way we verbalize our ideas and feelings during times of conflict makes all the difference. Here are five simple suggestions for maximizing the conflict-resolving process.

*Focus on one issue at a time.* We can't resolve one issue if someone keeps interjecting new ones. Resolving one conflict at a time is a challenge; resolving several at once is impossible. "Well, it's fine for you to talk about my leaving socks all over the house," a husband might say, "but how about the way you clip your fingernails in public!" He's guilty of what has been called "cross-complaining"—countering one complaint with another, instead of responding responsibly to the first.

*Deal with conflict before things reach the boiling point.* Lucy in "Peanuts" says her strategy is, "If I can't be right, I'll be wrong at the top of my lungs!" The phrase "lose your temper" is pretty accurate. Raising our voice in an explosion of anger may carry with it a feeling of raw power and may allow us to control the situation momentarily by sheer volume and aggression. But when we blow up, we've *lost* control, not gained it.

We must learn the early-warning signals of our anger and deal with conflict before it builds up enough pressure to "blow our tops." Otherwise, the explosion will usually discharge deadly verbal shrapnel—insults, accusations, profanity, threats, and the like.

*Open up and talk about it.* In his book *The Art of Understanding Yourself,* Dr. Cecil Osborne says that one of the ways men most often frustrate women is their refusal or inability to communicate, especially during conflict. Why are so many men that way? Probably because men tend to be more uncomfortable with emotions and less able to verbalize them. So men (women, too) often clam up, shut their feelings inside, and bury them alive. Silence can look quiet and noncombative, but in fact, be a way of punishing others by refusing to work toward resolution.

Talk about it. Express your grievances, your confusion, your pain. Others can't read your mind. Silence is ambiguous. What is he thinking? Is she still angry? What's that I don't hear you saying?

*Don't exaggerate.* We are surrounded by exaggerated claims—a laundry soap is a "washday miracle," a pulp novel is "the literary event of the decade." We must resist the temptation to do the same when stating our case in a conflict situation.

Overgeneralizations block resolution. "You never listen!" "You always make us late." "The only thing you care about is . . . " The moment the other person hears the exaggeration word ("never," "always," "only"), they can disregard our statement as unfair or offer an exception to our sweeping generalization. An exaggerated claim or grievance may seem to make our case sound stronger, but in fact an overstatement is a weaker statement. And it's not only ineffective, it's untrue.

*No cheap shots.* The better two people know each other, the more ways they know to make each other wince with a cheap shot to a vulnerable spot. Sometimes when we want to gain leverage in a discussion, we pull out the ace we've been hiding up our sleeves for just such a moment: "Oh, is that so? You weren't so smart the day you . . . "

Human beings are both the toughest and most fragile things God put on his earth. We need one another's protection, not exploitation. Cheap shots are against all the rules of resolution. Strike at someone's weak spot, and watch their defenses rise up, and the chances for resolution go down.

### Resolving from the Heart

Back in the late eighteenth century, a Delaware Indian chieftan named Tedynscung was told of Jesus Christ's teaching, "Do to others what you would have them do to you" (Matt. 7:12). He found it hard to accept. "It is impossible," he said. "It cannot be done. If the Great Spirit that made man would give him a new heart, he could do as you say, but not [otherwise]."

Conflict is inevitable in a world full of people, each of whom is uniquely different and is prone to want things "my way." But if God is at work within us, inwardly renewing us daily (2 Cor. 4:16), we have the new heart power—power to love and accept and forgive others as we would have them love and accept and forgive us, power to work past "my way" selfishness to "our way" resolutions.

[1] H. Norman Wright, *Training Christians to Counsel* (Denver: Christian Marriage Enrichment, 1977), p. 104

[2]Dietrich Bonhoeffer, "A Wedding Sermon from a Prison Cell," *Letters and Papers from Prison* (London: SCM Press Ltd., 1953, 1967, 1971) pp. 31-32. Reprinted with permission of the publisher.

[3]David Augsburger, *Caring Enough to Confront* (Scottdale, PA: Herald Press, 1980), pp. 12-22.

# 10

# *How to Be a*
# *People-Builder*

Growing up in West Texas meant that you constantly had to be on the watch for tornadoes. At my elementary school, we had regular tornado drills. An alarm bell would ring, and my class would huddle in the coat room for safety. We also had fire drills, in which we would march outside at the sound of a buzzer. One year I had a teacher who could never get the alarm signals straight. The fire buzzer would go off, and she would gather us into the coat room; the tornado bell would sound, and she would rush us outside! She always managed to make just the wrong response. Fortunately, there were no tornadoes or fires that year, or I probably would not have survived to tell the story.

While my befuddled teacher was good at making the *wrong* response, Jesus teaches us to be good at making the *right* response to people in their need. John says that Jesus "knew what was in a man." He knew what people's needs were, what made them tick. So his message was always right on target: for the poor, good news; for spiritual prisoners, freedom; for the blind, sight; for the oppressed, release (Luke 4:18). His gospel—and the church's gospel today—was and always must be *good* news. For our Father has what we need. "His divine power has given us *everything we need* for life and godliness" (2 Pet. 1:3).

125

### The Vitamin We Need

Appreciation and encouragement from others is a fundamental human need. A famous football coach tells the story on
himself about a vacation he and his family took in Maine. When
they walked into a movie theater and sat down, the handful of
people there applauded. "I can't believe it; people recognize me
all the way up here," he thought to himself. Then a man came
over to him and said, "Thanks for coming. They won't start the
movie for less than ten people."

We each need to be affirmed and built up, regular reminders
that we truly matter. Like a vitamin that our body must have but
cannot manufacture for itself, encouragement is something others must provide for us.

Even the Lord Jesus needed a validating word of encouragement now and again, and his Father gave it to him. At the
very beginning of his public ministry and again towards its end,
God affirmed him powerfully: "This is my Son, whom I love;
with him I am well-pleased" (Matt. 3:17 and 17:5). Surely this is
one of the most endearing and "fatherly" glimpses of God in all
scripture, speaking the words every son yearns to hear from his
father: "You're my son. I love you. I'm so proud of you."

Mark Twain's famous comment, "I can live for two months
on one good compliment," strikes a responsive chord in us all.
But while we must never underestimate the value of a sincere
compliment, our need is deeper than just for positive, flattering
words. We need someone to call us beyond mediocrity and
triviality to greater maturity, productivity, and vision. This is
what the writer of Hebrews was doing in his "word of exhortation"
(13:22) when he challenged Christians to "consider how we may
spur one another on toward love and good deeds" (10:24).

The gospel of God's grace is good news precisely because it
calls men and women to greatness—greatness as God counts it
(Mark 9:34-35). This is authentic encouragement: to affirm a
person's noble qualities and deeds, to deal honestly with his

counterproductive ideas and behavior, and to love him unconditionally through it all.

## Seldom Is Heard an Encouraging Word

A popular song expressed a common sentiment when it
begged, "sure could use a little good news today." Child psychologists write about an epidemic of inferiority among the
young. Where do people go for authentic encouragement today?
The contemporary secular value system seems to say with slick
persuasiveness, "You are a valuable human being *if* (and only
if) you are attractive, wealthy, athletic, brilliant, young, slim,
powerful, and sexy." The first problem with those standards is
that they encourage very few of us! The second problem is that
they are *false* standards of value. Those who meet those standards testify consistently and convincingly that such is not the
stuff that fills life to the full. Yet countless frustrated people buy
the lie and continue to measure their lives by standards that
pronounce most of them to be "second-rate," "unworthy," or
just "average."

One of our greatest statesmen was ridiculed by some of the
press of his day because of his accent and his looks: "a slang-
whanging stump speaker . . . a horrid-looking wretch . . . the
leanest, lankest, most ungainly mass of legs and arms and
hatchet face ever strung on a single frame." Such were some of
the editorial comments in 1860 on one Abraham Lincoln.

Ann Landers was once asked what single question was
asked most in the millions of letters she had received over the
many years of writing her column. It was the question: "What's
wrong with me?" Every time a child hears, "Can't you do
anything right?" he is handed a negative verdict on himself.
Every time a teenager exercises sexual restraint, peers are likely
to pronounce a negative verdict on him. Every time a cosmetic
ad airs, a million viewers receive a negative verdict—too fat, too
frizzy, too frumpy, too wrinkled, too grey, too ordinary. In a
world where low self-esteem is epidemic and seldom is heard a

truly encouraging word, many human beings have been wrongly convinced that their theme song is, "You're no good, you're no good, you're no good. Baby, you're no good!"

## God's Affirmative Word

But God is a God of affirmation, whose positive verdict on man was conclusively demonstrated in the sending of his Son (John 3:16, 1 John 4:9). *Jesus* is God's affirmative Word. "For no matter how many promises God has made, they are 'Yes' in Christ" (2 Cor. 1:20). Jesus is God's living and breathing message to us, and the message is yes! In him we hear the Father saying, "*Yes*, I love you unconditionally. *Yes*, I created you in my own image. *Yes*, I became one of you. *Yes*, I took every initiative and made the greatest sacrifice to make forgiveness and eternal life available to you. *Yes*, you are of infinite value! Would I have sent my only Son to a cross for you if it were not so?"

Elaborating on God's "yes" to us, Paul points to four affirmations in 2 Corinthians 1:21-22: "Now it is God who makes both us and you stand firm in Christ. He anointed us, set his seal of ownership on us, and put his Spirit in our hearts as a deposit, guaranteeing what is to come."

Picture this scene: You are an alien who has just fled from your repressive homeland. You now stand in a foreign immigration court, with no papers, no money, no friends or family. The judge asks, "Is there anyone who will sponsor this immigrant and stand by him?" A strong voice says, "Yes, I will." (He makes us stand firm.) "Will you give him a job commission?" "Yes." (He anoints us.) "Will you adopt him as your very own?" "Yes." (He sets his seal of ownership on us.) "And will you prove your good intention with a deposit to guarantee your promise?" "Yes, yes!" (He puts his Spirit in our hearts as a deposit.)

When God affirms and emancipates people in Christ, they are "no longer foreigners and aliens, but fellow citizens with God's people and members of God's household" (Eph. 2:19).

## The Distraction of Discouragement

"Little-faith" is the name of one of the Christian pilgrims in John Bunyan's classic allegory *Pilgrim's Progress.* On his way to the Celestial City, Little-faith is attacked and robbed by three rogues—Faint-heart, Mistrust, and Guilt. When he recovers, he finds that, while they took all his money, they overlooked his most precious possessions—his inheritance and his certificate of admission to the Celestial City. But Little-faith was devastated by the loss of his silver. Though he still had his inheritance and his certificate, all he could think and talk about was the robbery. He continued on his Christian pilgrimage, but from that time on he was a depressed, discouraged pilgrim.

Discouragement distracts us, shifts our attention away from God's most precious gifts and promises. Unchecked, it can rob us of our joy, our assurance, even our faith. In their wilderness wanderings the Israelites first whined and grew discouraged, then became faithless and rebellious. Most of them died in the desert. Against that stark historical backdrop, the writer of Hebrews counsels us, "encourage one another daily, as long as it is called Today, so that none of you may be hardened by sin's deceitfulness" (Heb. 3:13).

Sin has hoodwinked us when discouragement makes us forget the eternal security that God gives to members of his household. No loss of money, possessions, or prestige has to rob us of the eternal life within us. Don't invest your hearts too heavily in such commodities, Jesus advises (Matt. 6:19). "Why should I fear anything that cannot rob me of God," writes Thomas Merton, "and why should I desire anything that cannot give me possession of Him?"

## A Daily Minimum Requirement

Because discouragement can harden into sinfulness, we must take seriously the imperative to encourage one another daily. If encouragement is like a vitamin, then surely we each have a "daily minimum requirement" of its nurturing power.

Without it we too are in danger of growing faithless and rebellious.

I've heard some people express the fear that too much affirmation can make someone—especially a child—spoiled, egotistical, arrogant. I disagree. If your affirmation is sincere and constructive (not mere flattery), you cannot build up another person too much—especially a child. The egotist is seldom the person who has been loved and affirmed "too much." More often he is an insecure person overcompensating for his feelings of low self-esteem and self-worth.

God has affirmed us mightily. But he has given over the daily business of affirmation to his household, the church. Christian encouragement is a front-line defense against sin's deceitfulness. We need brothers and sisters who will both see the best in us and expect the best of us. Encouragement is a prime reason for our assemblies (Heb. 10:25).

The world needs to see the affirmative fellowship that Jesus established. On the cover of a book I have about famous preachers in history, not one of the two dozen pictured was smiling. What a sour bunch! Unfortunately, that is an image many have of Christians in general and preachers in particular. So much damage has been done by those sad souls whose religion has left them cold, fearful, neurotic, or hypercritical. Those with eyes fixed on Jesus are the gospel messengers, the good-news people with an encouraging word for a discouraged world.

But how does this vitamin, this all-important mutual encouragement work? Two key New Testament terms define the process. The two "encouragement-words" are *edification* and *exhortation*.

### Edification: A People-Building Process

In his exceptional work *Mere Christianity*, C. S. Lewis asks you, the reader, to imagine yourself as a living house that God has come to rebuild. At first he does the minor repairs you expected but then he starts making major alterations—new wings, extra floors, grand towers, and beautiful courtyards! You discover that his intention is to make of you a palace fit for him to inhabit.

The Greek word for "edify" (*oikodomeō*) means literally "to build a house."[1] Spiritual growth is often likened in scripture to the construction of a building (Matt. 7:24-25, Eph. 2:19-22). As we attend to the building of our own houses "upon the rock," we are needed on one another's construction sites as well. "Therefore, encourage one another and *build each other up*" (1 Thess. 5:11). In this building project that is Christ's church, we need every carpenter, painter, welder, and electrician whom we can enlist. We bolster. We repair. We protect. We equip. God calls me to see your "edifice" as my concern. "Let us therefore make every effort to do what leads to peace and to mutual edification" (Rom. 14:19).

A brief look at some of the contexts in which Paul used the term "edify" or "build up" demonstrates that people-building requires patience, graciousness, and personal discipline:

*Romans 15:1-3.* We build one another up by gently bearing with the failings of weak brothers and sisters.

*1 Corinthians 8:1-2.* We build one another up with our sensitive love more than with our arrogant knowledge.

*1 Corinthians 10:23-24.* We build one another up by not flaunting our freedom in Christ.

But what is our objective? Our ultimate objective is to "present everyone perfect (mature) in Christ" (Col. 1:28), to "become mature, attaining to the whole measure of the fulness of Christ" (Eph. 4:13). It is no small service to help others work through problems with family, weight, dating, or self-image. But if we only lift their spirits or boost their egos, have we helped them grow more into the image of Jesus? Paul's strongest criticism of the exercise of spiritual gifts in Corinth was that they were being used for *self*-edification and not mutual edification. "Since you are eager to have spiritual gifts, try to excel in gifts that *build up* the church" (1 Cor. 14:12). The greatest people-builder is he or she who equips others for the service of God.

## Exhortation: A Comforting Process

An extraordinary servant in the early church was named Joseph, but apparently no one called him that. Rather, he was known as Barnabas, a wonderful nickname meaning "Son of Encouragement" or "Son of Exhortation" (Acts 4:36). The word for "exhort" *(parakaleō)* from which his name was derived can also be translated "comfort," "entreat," or "encourage." It literally means to call someone to your side, for the purpose of giving assistance.[2] We speak of the trusted friends who "stand by us" or "stick with us" in our hour of need. Barnabas was that kind of Christian brother.

Philippians 2 begins, "If you have any encouragement from being united with Christ, . . . " Paul seems to say here that being in Christ means that we can count on an unfailing source of encouragement. We stand by one another every day (Heb. 3:13). The supply line of our encouragement runs directly to the Father, whom Paul described as "the God of all comfort *(paraklēsis)*, who comforts us in our troubles, so that we can comfort those in any trouble with the comfort we ourselves have received from God" (2 Cor. 1:3-4).

Drawing upon our own resources, we quickly become discouraged encouragers, exhausted exhorters. But if the Spirit of the God of all comfort lives in us, our resources are mighty. Jesus gave the Holy Spirit a unique name, the *Paraclete*, "the Comforter" (KJV) or "the Counselor" (NIV). As he described the comfort of God's Spirit in John 14-16, we catch a glimpse of what the process of exhortation involves.

First, Jesus called him "the Spirit of truth" (14:17, 15:26, 16:13). A true comforter deals honestly with others' problems and struggles, and points others to God's truth that sets men free (John 8:32). Elders encourage the church by healthy teaching or sound doctrine (Tit. 1:9). Paul writes of "the encouragement of the Scriptures" (Rom. 15:4).

Second, the Paraclete's function is to remind men of Jesus' teachings (14:26) and to testify about the Lord (15:26). A true

**66**

This is authentic
encouragement: to
affirm a person's noble qualities,
to deal openly with his self-defeating
behavior, and to love him
unconditionally
through it all.

**99**

Christian comforter points others to Jesus and to the great hope he offers. Paul told the Thessalonians about his glorious second coming, then instructed, "encourage each other with these words" (1 Thess. 4:18).

Third, the Spirit's comfort is the peace of the Lord, not the elusive and insubstantial peace the world offers (14:27). The true comforter offers not humanistic bandages for life's deepest wounds, but the concrete healing of God's forgiveness. Peter's powerful words on the day of Pentecost were not so much to comfort gently, but to plead urgently with men to be saved: "he *pleaded* (*parakaleō*) with them, 'Save yourselves from this corrupt generation' " (Acts 2:40).

Finally, the Spirit of truth, the Counselor, will, like Jesus, be with us forever (14:16-18). A true comforter will never forsake another, just as God has promised us, "Never will I leave you; never will I forsake you" (Heb. 13:5). When Solomon speaks of "a friend who sticks closer than a brother" (Prov. 18:24), he aptly describes the beautiful Barnabases in the kingdom of God.

## The Encouragement of Assembly

"Let us not give up meeting together, as some are in the habit of doing, but let us encourage one another—and all the more as you see the Day approaching" (Heb. 10:25). Some Christians had begun to "forsake the assembly" of the saints. Why? It could be that the heat of persecution was taking its toll or that the newness of their faith had simply worn off. Perhaps they did not feel that fellowship with God required fellowship with other believers. Or perhaps they just did not wish to be encumbered with the many needs, problems, and responsibilities that go along with being a Christian family. Whatever was keeping them away, the inspired writer called for their return with this simple appeal: we need one another's encouragement!

We assemble not to receive credit for church attendance, but to encourage one another. Our assembly times provide choice opportunities to build one another up, to "spur one another on toward love and good deeds" (Heb. 10:24). What goes on before and after a worship service—the sharing, the laughter, the comforting, the admonishing—are no less "spiritual" than what goes on during the service. The fellowship out of which authentic encouragement blossoms is not one of faith's "luxury options" like white sidewalls or power windows; it is very much a "standard feature" of the kingdom. "If we walk in the light, as he is in the light, we have fellowship with one another" (1 John 1:7). When we forsake the assembly we do not forsake a mere event or requirement; we forsake one another. And we miss out on prime encouragement time.

But someone invariably says, "I don't always receive that encouragement when I come to church." We have all felt that way, surely. And that's all the more reason to heed the writer of Hebrews, who is not asking, "Are you receiving the encouragement you need?" but rather, "Are you *offering* the encouragement others need?" You can control only one Christian in this world: yourself. And God calls you to be an encourager, a people-builder, a comforter, "and all the more as you see the Day approaching."

## Saying Yes to One Another

In Christ God has said yes to us, and now wills to say his yes through us. Verbalizing our affirmation of one another is not only a joyous privilege, but it is also a difficult responsibility. Many people find critical words much easier to express than encouraging ones. Paul exhibited a great gift for verbal encouragement in his letters, as in Romans 16, where he communicated warm greetings and expressions of love to a long list of brothers and sisters. Here are some practical dos and don'ts of Christian people-building:

*Move beyond polite formalities.* Proper etiquette teaches us pleasant words to say to one another: "Good to see you." "You're looking well." "We had a good time." But social pleasantries do not build up people like sincere, substantive words of encouragement. C. S. Lewis rightly asserted that Christians are more than just nice people; they are new men and women.

*Be specific.* Criticism is not only more prevalent than encouragement, it is usually more specific as well. In building up one another we are helped most by comments that are not "global," but rather encourage the further growth and expression of specific attitudes, spiritual gifts, or behavior. When Paul made his typical expression of thanksgiving at the beginning of most of his epistles, he made it a point to identify precisely what he was thankful for (See Eph. 1:15-16, Col. 1:3-8).

*Never manipulate with affirmation.* With some persons, an encouraging word is invariably followed by a request. Our cynical world has come to expect a "hook" with every compliment. True encouragement is distinguished from flattery by its lack of ulterior motives. To "butter up" or "soft-soap" another is exploitative and counterfeit affirmation.

*Give clear signals.* Don't mix words of encouragement with oblique or sarcastic comments: "You do pretty well for your age." "I can't believe you did such a good job." Communicate your edification in direct and unmistakable language, so the other won't have to wonder, "How did he mean that?" Express your good words directly to the person who needs it, not indirectly through others. People-building works best person-to-person.

*Write messages of affirmation.* When we are not able to speak face-to-face, written messages are an excellent alternative, with unique advantages. Some shy persons are accused, as Paul, of being "timid when face to face with you, but bold when away" (2 Cor. 10:1). As a result they express themselves better in writing than in person. Also, a written word of encouragement can be kept, cherished, and re-read. It can be an ongoing building-block in someone's life.

## A Final Blessing

A popular and effective minister suffered a nervous breakdown. Nothing, it seemed, could lift him out of his depression. One day a friend suggested this therapy: Identify some people who have had a positive impact on your life and write them a simple thank-you note. The minister thought of a school teacher who early in his life had instilled in him a love of learning. He wrote her and expressed his thankfulness. Some time later a letter arrived from the woman, long since retired: "You have warmed my old heart. I have taught school for fifty years. Yours is the first letter of thanks I ever received from a student, and I shall cherish it until I die." The minister went on to write some five hundred such letters of thanks; his "encouragement-therapy" played a major role in working his way back from a crippling despondency.[3]

People-building has a wonderful residual benefit: it builds us up as well. It develops in us a keen eye for the true, the noble, the lovely, the admirable, the praiseworthy (Phil. 4:8). Offering the essential daily vitamin of encouragement tunes our hearts to the needs of our neighbors, develops in us eyes of compassion and sensitivity. Words of exhortation and edification are powerful enhancers of "the tie that binds our hearts in Christian love," key terms in the lexicon of Christian body language.

[1]W. E. Vine, "Edification, Edify, Edifying," *An Expository Dictionary of New Testament Words* (Old Tappan, NJ: Fleming H. Revell Co., 1940), 2, pp. 24-25.

[2]Vine, "Exhort, Exhortation," *Expository Dictionary,* 2, p. 60.

[3]James Christensen, *Don't Waste Your Time in Worship* (Old Tappan, NJ: Fleming H. Revell CO., 1978), p. 23.

# 11

# *Caring Enough to Correct*

Most of us have witnessed this bit of American sports drama: an angry baseball manager and an umpire stand toe to toe and nose to nose, loudly arguing whether the man was safe or out. That scene is a fair representation of the original meaning of the English word "confront." It means literally, "foreheads together"! Thus we speak of a "head-to-head confrontation."

Have you ever been confronted? Your boss or co-worker or spouse or parents or friend or somebody you don't even know says to you, "You blew it!" Now, umpires get that kind of treatment all the time; they are supposed to be thick-skinned. But how do you feel when confronted? Embarrassed, perhaps? Defensive? Guilty? Surprised? Angry, at yourself and/or at the person who confronts you?

Why do we typically react negatively to confrontation? Here are four possible reasons: first, none of us enjoys having his weaknesses and shortcomings placed under a spotlight. A wound to the ego hurts, and so, quite naturally, we flinch. Second, sometimes a confrontation is painful because the spirit of the other person is haughty and insensitive. Third, sometimes the person does not have his facts straight, and his indictment of us is unfair. And fourth, sometimes the problem is solely our own—we are just not open to the possibility that we can be wrong and need correction.

The community of people that Jesus Christ established—his church—is to be like the man who said, "I dropped a rock on my big toe, and my whole body stayed up all night to keep my aching toe company!" Because following Jesus means belonging to his body, whose members are responsible for one another (Rom. 12:5), it is crucial that we honestly examine our attitudes toward what scripture calls "admonition." We aren't to be a group of "garbage collectors" or "sin detectors" searching out imperfections in one another. Christian love keeps no record of wrongs and does not delight in evil (1 Cor. 13:5-6). But we are in Christ a living body showing tender concern for every individual part (1 Cor. 12:25).

## What Is Admonition?

The Greek word translated "admonish" (*noutheteo*) can also be translated "warn," "advise," "instruct" or "counsel." It does not refer to teaching in the sense of imparting information; neither does it mean to chastise or criticize. Rather, it carries the meaning of "setting the mind (or heart) aright"—to redirect or encourage a person toward a correct behavior or attitude.[1]

The apostle Paul is the source of the word *noutheteo* each time it occurs in the New Testament. He sees admonition as everyone's responsibility:

*Elders, apostles, and other church leaders:* those "who are over you in the Lord and who *admonish* you" (1 Thess. 5:12). Paul told his beloved Ephesian elders "I never stopped *warning* each of you night and day with tears" (Acts 20:31). And he described his ministry this way to the Colossians: "We proclaim him, *admonishing* and teaching everyone with all wisdom, so that we may present everyone perfect in Christ" (Col. 1:28).

*Parents:* "Fathers, do not exasperate your children; instead, bring them up in the training and *instruction* of the Lord" (Eph. 6:4).

*The entire church:* "Let the word of Christ dwell in you richly as you teach and *admonish* one another with all wisdom" (Col. 3:16). Paul praises the maturity of Christians in Rome who are "full of goodness, complete in knowledge and competent to *instruct* one another" (Rom. 15:14).

So confrontation is appropriate within the body of Christ. But how do we do admonish each other and still avoid what Paul strictly cautions Christians against: "Let us stop passing judgment on one another" (Rom. 14:13)? We must look carefully for biblical guidelines.

## The Right Circumstance for Admonition

When is it correct for a Christian to admonish others? Let's use Galatians 6:1-2 as a guide. "Brothers, if someone is caught in a sin, you who are spiritual should restore him gently. But watch yourself, or you also may be tempted. Carry each other's burdens, and in this way you will fulfull the law of Christ."

First, admonition is right when a Christian brother or sister needs our aid because they have been "caught in a sin." The exact meaning of this phrase is uncertain. Either the person has been caught up or involved in ongoing sinful behavior, or we have discovered their transgression firsthand. In either case, we know about their weakness and have a responsibility to them to help with that burden.

If the sin is against us personally, Jesus advises us to follow these steps as necessary: The first step is always to speak with the fellow Christian personally. If there is no resolution, go again to him, this time with one or two other Christians. If still no change results, bring the problem before the church family. Finally, when all else fails, avoid him altogether (Matt. 18:15-17).

Clearly, Jesus' primary concern is to protect the spiritual life of the sinning brother, to "win him over." You go directly to him—no gossip, no character assassination—and verbalize your concern privately. Next, bring in other Christians, not to build a stronger case for yourself but to be objective and to protect your brother's interests. Their wisdom may help bring about a resolution. (They may even find that you are in the wrong!) Failing in that, seek the collective judgment of the church family, assuming the matter is one that should be made public. Only as a last resort in your efforts to win him back, break fellowship with him.

The commentator William Barclay contends that this passage is "too legalistic to be a saying of Jesus." Quite the contrary. Here Jesus is protecting the weak believer against unfair accusation, judgment, and premature expulsion from the fellowship.

Sometimes church discipline may be necessary in cases such as the flagrant case of sexual immorality at Corinth (1 Cor. 5:1-5), where individual behavior damages the church's public reputation. Another sin against the body of Christ that scripture targets for swift admonition is divisiveness: "*Warn* a divisive person once, and then *warn* him a second time. After that, have nothing to do with him" (Tit. 3:10).

## The Right Person for Admonition

Next, admonition is right when a "spiritual" person goes to the one trapped in sin. Who qualifies as a "spiritual" person? Is Paul suggesting that only a sinless person should "throw the first stone"? Who then can admonish? For an understanding of the kind of spirituality Paul is thinking of, look at his description of those Christians whom he considered to be "competent to instruct [admonish] one another" (Rom. 15:14).

He says they were, first, "full of goodness"—they were making every effort themselves to live Christ-like lives. In Jesus' words, they were spiritually mature enough to make sure that they had removed the "plank" from their own eye before trying to remove the "speck of sawdust" from their brother's eye (Matt. 7:3-5).

They were "complete in knowledge"—they had a mature understanding of God's will. Our competence to admonish means a commitment to the authority of scripture that helps us distinguish between biblical absolutes and non-absolutes. The Word of God—not church traditions, not social norms, not my personal preferences—must be the basis for any confrontation.

A healthy spiritual balance of these two traits, goodness and knowledge, creates the right atmosphere for effective admonition. Knowledge provides the necessary biblical perspective and correction. And goodness protects the vulnerable spirit not only of the weaker brother, but also of the confronting person ("watch yourself").

**The Right Goal**

Finally, admonition is right when its goal is to restore the person gently. Have you ever restored something? The old piano that sits in our dining room was pink (yes, pink) when we got it. Carefully, slowly, we removed the bright paint, then sanded, stained, and varnished it until the original beauty of the wood was restored. Christians are people involved in a constant process of restoration. Paul called it "being renewed day by day" (2 Cor. 4:16). So restoration is a natural and essential dynamic of "new creation" life.

But let us not miss the crucial spirit that sets mature Christian confrontation apart: *gentleness.* Gentleness is a fruit of the Holy Spirit (Gal. 5:23), a mark of Christ-likeness (2 Cor. 10:1). "Handle with care," Paul is saying "Your role is to restore, not to ravage; to put things right, not to punish." We can hear this concern in his gentle words to the erring Corinthians: "I am not writing this to shame you, but to *warn* you, as my dear children" (1 Cor. 4:14).

John R. W. Stott calls Galatians 6:1-2 the New Testament answer to Cain's sullen question, "Am I my brother's keeper?" (Gen. 4:9). The answer is *yes.* If a man is my brother in Christ, then I am his keeper.

**Judge Not**

"Do not judge, or you too will be judged" (Matt. 7:1) is one of Jesus' most abused sayings. Translated by many people it means, "Mind your own business! Get off my case!" But is that what he meant? A purely literal interpretation of "judge not" could have Jesus prohibiting all courts of law, all justice, even all laws.

Of course we must learn to make discerning judgments, using God's Word as our standard. As Friedrich Buchsel notes, Matthew 7:1 "does not imply flabby indifference to the moral condition of others." Rather, it is our Lord's warning to the faultfinder, the religious watchdog whose self-appointed task is to judge everyone around him. This "judge" has an eye for failure and weakness, reads the worst motives into others' actions, and goes about his work with little mercy. He tends to be long on confrontation but short on servanthood.

Such ungracious judgment usurps the place of God, the only Judge who sees through to the heart. Measured by a coldly judgmental eye, King David does poorly. (At best, he made only a 60% score on the Ten Commandments!) His influence might have been dismissed; instead, he became the forerunner of the Messiah, who would be the "son of David." His psalms might have been discredited; instead, he is the best-loved devotional voice for believers through the ages. God looked into the heart of this imperfect king and loved what he saw: "a man after his own heart" (1 Sam. 13:14, 16:7).

## Peter: A Study in Correctability

Simon Peter had many excellent qualities that made him a great servant of God: his leadership, his frankness, his energy, his devotion. But one quality in particular helped Peter grow into the nickname Jesus gave him: "the Rock." Peter was *correctable*. Only the correctable person benefits from admonition.

On at least eight different occasions, the Bible tells us, the fisherman from Capernaum openly "blew it." He faltered and sank on the Sea of Galilee (Matt. 14:28-31). He rebuked Jesus for talking about his death (Matt. 16:22-23). He spoke out of turn at the Transfiguration (Matt. 17:4-5). He initially refused to let Jesus wash his feet (John 13:6-10). He went to sleep with the others in Gethsemane (Matt. 26:40-41). He cut off the ear of Malchus at Jesus' arrest (John 18:10-11). He denied any relation-

**66**

*Setting the mind (or heart) aright.*

**99**

ship with Jesus during the trial (Luke 22:54-62). He practiced racial discrimination against his Gentile brothers at Antioch (Gal. 2:11-14).

Each time he failed, Peter received some kind of admonition, usually verbal—from Paul, from Jesus, from God. Can you imagine the humiliation he must have felt—scrambling wet and sputtering back into the boat, or having Jesus call him "Satan"? Or later, hearing the ominous crow of the rooster and having his Lord look straight at him?

But Peter was not one to be defeated by his moments of weakness. No pouting, no angry retaliations, and no attempts to rationalize his behavior are recorded. He received his admonition, felt his shame, cried his bitter and penitent tears, then pressed on in his Master's service. What a noble spirit of correctability! That is why it was Peter who could speak the church's bold inaugural address on Pentecost. That is why it was Peter who could give us these powerful, credible words: "Clothe yourselves with humility toward one another, because, 'God opposes the proud but gives grace to the humble.' Humble yourselves, therefore, under God's mighty hand, that he may lift you up in due time" (1 Peter 5:5-6).

## The Correctable Person

A person's attitude toward correction depends in large part on his view of the church. If someone goes to church for much the same reasons that he goes to the store (to get a product he likes) or goes to the theater (to play a spectator role), predictably he will resist admonition. After all, you probably wouldn't grant most people you run into at the grocery or the movies the right to question your values or behavior, would you?

Who then does have the right to correct us? The New Testament tells us that the best choice is a fellow disciple of Jesus. If I must be admonished, let it be by one who is committed to help bear my burdens, not increase them. Let it be by one who shares equally my joys *and* my tears. Let it be by one who will never gossip about me or shame me. Let it be by one who is more concerned with the planks in his own eye than the specks in mine. And let it be by one who, when he confronts me, does so gently and humbly.

In short, the person who has the right to admonish me is the mature Christian brother or sister who approaches me within the context of two spiritual *relationships* which have already been firmly established—with the Lord Jesus and with me. Within the security of those relationships I can dare to trust, dare to be vulnerable, dare to confess my sins (James 5:16).

Paul devoted considerable space in Romans to admonishing the church family to be accepting and gracious with "weak" persons: "Accept him whose faith is weak, without passing judgment on disputable matters" (14:1). "Each of us will give an account of himself to God. Therefore let us stop passing judgment on one another" (14:12-13). "We who are strong ought to bear with the failings of the weak and not to please ourselves" (15:1). "Accept one another, then, just as Christ accepted you, in order to bring praise to God" (15:7).

The Servant Messiah foretold by Isaiah was to be one who would be gentle with the weak: "A bruised reed he will not break, and a smoldering wick he will not snuff out" (42:3). Jesus took sin with "deadly seriousness"; he came to call us out of our sin and weakness. But along the pathway to Christian maturity he shows us—and asks that we show one another—great patience, acceptance, and compassion.

## Our Precious Freedom in Christ

Jesus invited people to find in him freedom and rest from the burdens of legalistic religion (Matt. 11:28-30), and strictly forbade a spirit of judgmentalism (Matt. 7:1-2). Jesus' keynote address in his hometown synagogue was a spiritual emancipation proclamation: "The Spirit of the Lord is on me . . . to proclaim freedom for the prisoners . . . to release the oppressed" (Luke 4:18). Paul, whom F. F. Bruce has fittingly called "the apostle of the heart set free," writes, "where the Spirit of the

Lord is, there is freedom" (2 Cor. 3:17), and again, "It is for freedom that Christ has set us free" (Gal. 5:1).

In a harshly demanding and judgmental world, the church is a refuge of grace and acceptance, populated by men and women living in the rich climate of God's mercy (Eph. 2:4-8). That climate is polluted whenever we begin to bind on fellow Christians any doctrines, life-style expectations, modes of worship, or methods of ministry not mandated by scripture. Within the one body of Christ we should expect to see great diversity in gifts and styles of service (1 Cor. 12:1-31). Our individual spiritual freedoms are a precious and gracious gift from God and must be not only granted but carefully guarded.

Among the churches in Galatia, false teachers attempted to bind on Christians the Jewish rite of circumcision and other legalistic demands. Paul resisted this influence as strongly as anything he ever encountered. "You, my brothers, were called to be *free*," he writes (Gal. 5:13). Notice, however, that he quickly adds, "But do not use your freedom to indulge your sinful nature." Our greatest freedom of all in Christ is our freedom from the curse of sin (Rom. 6:2-7, 22-23).

## Room to Grow

In the Basilica of St. John Lateran in Rome stand massive statues of the apostles, each on a high pedestal. Master sculptors have depicted them as muscular, handsome men, almost godlike in appearance. But in all likelihood the apostles were quite ordinary looking; they probably resembled you and me more than Superman. What made them great was their willingness to be shaped and corrected by the Master. And so erratic Peter became a rock. John, one of the "sons of thunder," became the apostle of love. Doubting Thomas became a believer.

Each of them had their moments of weakness. But they grew stronger, because they realized that they had so much room to grow. And when the necessary admonitions came, they listened. And repented. And grew.

We have no right to impose human standards on one

another, but we do have the responsibility to admonish one another to return to the standards of the kingdom of God that are clearly stated in his authoritative word.

Each one of us will, more than once, become the "weaker" brother. When those times come, let us pray that we find ourselves surrounded by Christians who are both "full of goodness" and "complete in knowledge," who care enough to correct us when we need it, and who love and accept us all the while. And, when those times come, let us pray that we ourselves will be correctable.

[1]J. Behm, "vouθετέw" *Theological Dictionary of the New Testament,* Gerhard Kittel, ed. (Grand Rapids: Wm. B. Eerdmans Publishing Company, 1967), IV, 1019-1022; Friedel Selter, "Exhort," *The New International Dictionary of New Testament Theology,* Colin Brown, ed. (Grand Rapids: Zondervan Publishing House, 1975), I, pp. 567-569.

# 12

## The Torchbearers

Countless Americans in 1984 were stirred at the sight of the Olympic torch being carried through communities across this country on its way to Los Angeles. Then millions of us watched on television as Rafer Johnson mounted a seemingly endless succession of steps, paused for a dramatic moment, and then with that small flame lighted the huge torch at the Los Angeles Coliseum.

That exciting picture is reminiscent of a scene from antiquity: when the Greek victory messenger would arrive in town, assemble the people in the marketplace, raise his right hand and shout, "Rejoice! We are victorious!" The Greeks had a special word for the news of victory he brought: *euangelion*, the good news, the gospel.

### Raising the Torch

Combine those images and you get an important biblical picture: the Christian as a torchbearer. He or she brings good news to the marketplace, news of spiritual victory. The very Source of Light himself gave his followers clear instructions on how to bring his light to the marketplaces of the world: "You are the light of this world. I do not give you your light so you may hide it under cover, but so that you may raise it high among the people and give light to all. For when that torch is shining, your good deeds and good news will light the way for men to come to know God" (See Matt. 5:14-16).

How do I best communicate my faith? How can I be an effective messenger of victory, a bringer of good news? That's a question which confronts every believer. For Jesus did not say to his disciples, "I encourage some of you to attempt to have the impact of salt and light on your world." Rather, he said to them all: "You *are* the salt of the earth. . . . You *are* the light of the world" (Matt. 5:13-14). He handed a torch to every follower.

But most of us struggle with the role of torchbearer, don't we? "I don't know what to say." "I feel so awkward, so unnatural, trying to be evangelistic." "I'm not sure it's my gift." "I don't want to sound phony or fanatical and turn someone off." Some of our reluctance may stem from a timidity that we need to overcome (2 Tim. 1:7). But we may be pulling back because we have seen too many evangelistic attempts that were neither sensitive nor sensible. We rightly do not want to be guilty of the evangelistic malpractice that has caused so many in our time to tune out virtually any religious message.

### Earning a Hearing

More religious content is being communicated to more people today than ever before. In an average week the number of Americans who hear a religious message by radio or television is greater than the number who attend a church service. A 1984 Gallup survey found that 13.5 million people in this country watch at least fifteen minutes of religious programming weekly. Television evangelists have become national celebrities—"Stars of the Cathode Church," *Time* dubbed them.

Ironically, much of today's skepticism and unresponsiveness toward the Christian message may in large part stem from the high visibility of so many religious messengers. So many offer oversimplified answers and guaranteed blessings, all the while prodding, "Keep us on the air. . . . Send us a check. . . .

Support our latest facility/satellite/enterprise. . . . We need your prayers and your money. . . . "

As much as ever before, Christians must *earn* a hearing for the good news. Many of our neighbors have been "burned" by a distorted message or a manipulative messenger. The beauty of Jesus' personality and gospel has been tragically obscured by human egos and empires. Listeners' trust has to be rebuilt, communication lines repaired and reopened. Old approaches to evangelism need careful reevaluation.

Jesus gave his people a Great Commission (Matt. 28:19-20); it must not be abandoned simply because of the evangelistic indiscretions of some. We are his torchbearers. It is not enough for us simply to condemn methods we find distasteful or downright unbiblical. We must be looking for positive, natural ways to hold up the torch in the marketplace. With that resolve, let's look carefully at both the torch and its bearer.

## The Torch: The Gospel

For one hundred years a famous lady has stood in the New York Harbor, her upraised torch promising liberty to all those who come to her shores. Christians likewise raise a torch of liberty.

The torch we bear is the gospel of our Lord Jesus. This "good news" was the theme of his earliest recorded preaching (Mark 1:14-15). But what exactly is this gospel? Many religious messages have been billed as "gospel preaching." We must exercise the greatest of care that we define "gospel" biblically; for Paul directed his strongest outrage at the man who tampered with the message: "let him be eternally condemned!" (Gal. 1:8-9).

Paul opens his letter to the Romans, which some have called "the gospel according to Paul," by giving a thorough description of the Christian gospel. Look carefully at Romans 1:1-17. Notice how the apostle begins by saying that he was "set apart" for this gospel (1:1). Originally a member of the Pharisees (a name meaning the "set-apart ones"), Paul had set himself apart for the law. But God set him apart for the gospel!

In this passage we can learn to recognize the authentic gospel by some key characteristics:

*Origin:* "the gospel of God" (1:1). The early Anglo-Saxon word "Godspell" meant "God-story." The gospel is first and foremost a message from and about the Father, revealed to man through his Son, the Living Word, and his scriptures, the written word.

*Continuity:* "the gospel he promised beforehand through the prophets in the Holy Scriptures" (1:2). The Old Testament is not second-rate scripture to the Christian. It is Volume I of the good news, and deserves to be taught and preached as such.

*Subject:* "his Son . . . Jesus Christ our Lord" (1:3,4). In what may be his last surviving epistle, Paul sums up his gospel for Timothy. After countless sermons, classes, and personal conversations about the gospel, he boiled it down to this: "Remember *Jesus Christ,* raised from the dead, descended from David. *This is my gospel . . .* " (2 Tim. 2:8). If Jesus is not the unmistakable center of our proclamation, it will never be what scripture calls "the gospel."

*Purpose:* "to call people from among all the Gentiles to the obedience that comes from faith" (1:5). The good news was intended to be a global message; "among all the Gentiles" is another way of saying "among all nations of the world." As the world hears, faith will be born. And as faith grows, obedience will follow. Thus John describes the purpose of his Gospel: "that you may believe . . . , and that by believing you may have life in his name" (John 20:31).

*Power:* "the gospel . . . is the power of God" (1:16). When the gospel is biblically defined and clearly communicated, it is powerful! God himself is working in it to change lives, to save believers, to reveal his righteousness. He takes the seed of faith and makes it grow (1 Cor. 3:6). The power is in God's gospel, not the evangelist; in the news, not the newsboy; in the torch, not the torchbearer.[1]

## The Bearer: A Witness

Jesus' first public words were about the gospel. And final words to his followers were, "you will be my *witnesses* in Jerusalem, and in all Judea and Samaria, and to the ends of the earth" (Acts 1:8).

In court, a witness is sworn to speak truthfully about what he has firsthand knowledge of. To do otherwise is to "bear false witness." A crucial component in our torchbearing is the *personalizing* of the message; that is, it must be *my* gospel, *my* good news. Paul wrote of "my gospel" (2 Tim. 2:8). Now did he mean to suggest that it was his invention, or a message centered in himself? Quite the contrary; we have already noted his strong condemnation of "other gospels" (Gal. 1:6-9). Rather, it had become part of his life's story, his personal history—just as the Exodus was (and still is) relived by the Jews at Passover: "We were slaves of Pharaoh in Egypt, but the Lord brought us out . . . "

Have you ever seen this happen? A professional quarterback—strong, skilled, well-paid—fades back to pass. He spots a receiver far downfield in the open. He plants his back foot, brings his arm forward with a powerful motion, and . . . What happens? Nothing. Because a big defensive lineman just slapped the ball right out of his hand. As with the quarterback, so it is with a Christian witness: *you cannot pass on what you do not have.*

An Amy Grant song says, "It's not a song till it touches your heart." Being a witness means having an eternal song in my heart, having a biblical message that is being internalized and personalized. I can teach a doctrine that is God's eternal truth, but until that truth invigorates *my* conscience and nurtures *my* joy, I will probably find it difficult to share with much sincere enthusiasm. For it has not yet become "my gospel."

## Communicating the Gospel According to the Gospel

The church at Corinth had been "evangelized" not only by Paul but also by some false teachers who opposed his leadership.

So in 2 Corinthians Paul counters their influence by identifying some distorted approaches to evangelism. Among them:

*The Peddler* (2 Cor. 2:17). Wine-sellers and innkeepers were notorious back then for watering down their wine to enhance profits, so the term "wine-seller" became synonymous with deceptive peddlers and money-hungry hucksters who would sell a watered-down product. Paul was no "peddler" and his gospel was no "product" to be marketed by human salesmanship for human profit. Do we sometimes "water down" the Christian message? The story is told of some of the first missionaries to China, who left the crucifixion scene out of the life of Jesus because the Orientals found it so shocking! Sincerity is the style of "men sent from God," Paul says. So we do not peddle the gospel, but witness to it in all honesty and in all its fullness.

*The Self-Proclaimer* (2 Cor. 4:5). Getting ourselves out of the way so others can see and respond to Jesus is one of the toughest tasks we messengers face. But people will never be converted to Christ—become "Christians"—until it is Christ they hear proclaimed. Faith must rest on God and his power, not on any messenger's eloquence, wisdom, or persuasiveness (1 Cor. 2:1-5). As James Denney put it so beautifully, "No man can give at once the impression that he is clever and that Christ is mighty to save."

*The Trickster* (2 Cor. 4:2). I recall as a teenager working on a weekend evangelistic campaign effort. We went door-to-door, telling people we were taking a religious survey. But we weren't, not really. We were trying to arrange Bible studies, and the "survey" questions were just part of a "foot-in-the-door" technique, a pretext for leading people into a discussion about their religious habits. No great crime, perhaps, but a subtle deception nonetheless. We must use every ounce of ingenuity and creativity we have to get past the "watchful dragons" that prevent people from giving the gospel a fair hearing. But we must take scrupulous care not to become, even unintentionally, tricksters who mask their real agenda and message.

**66**

*A crucial component
in our torchbearing is our
personal message; that is, it
must be my gospel,
my good news*

**99**

## When Evangelism Becomes Manipulative

When a person's soul is at stake, isn't any method of evangelism right if it "works"? No. A good end does not justify a deceptive means. "We do not use deception, nor do we distort the word of God. On the contrary, by setting forth the truth plainly we commend ourselves to every man's conscience in the sight of God" (2 Cor. 4:2). We must respect every person's God-given free will. "Any persuasive effort which restricts another's freedom to choose for or against Jesus Christ is wrong," writes Em Griffin in his book *The Mind Changers*.

It is one thing to persuade—to set forth an intelligent, convicting case for the Christian faith, appealing both to head and heart. Paul said clearly, "We try to persuade men" (2 Cor. 5:11). But manipulation is another matter. Manipulation happens when a person is caused to accept a belief or perform an action without having made a reasonably informed decision to do so.

Here are some conditions under which religious manipulation can take place:

*Conditional Love and Friendship.* Have you ever enjoyed someone's friendly attentions, then found out that this was just his or her way of "setting you up" for a sales pitch? The love we express to others must be sincere and genuine (Rom. 12:9), never conditional upon their degree of receptiveness to our evangelistic efforts. A practice sometimes called "love-bombing" has been observed among many cultic groups. A person is smothered with attention and affection when he first comes into the group. Later he is threatened or punished with the withholding of that affection if he does not conform to group expectations. Christian love is never used as a control device.

*Arbitrary Goals and Quotas.* Setting personal or congregational goals for spiritual growth is not only useful but essential. But there are inherent dangers in arbitrarily setting a goal for someone's conversion ("by January 1") or for a church's evangelistic success ("fifty baptisms this year"). Such goals and quotas can exert an unnatural pressure on individual Christians—to "produce"—and on potential converts. I cringe when I hear someone say, "I intend to be married by age twenty-five"; his artificial timetable could pressure him into a disastrously premature or ill-considered decision. So it is with one's coming to faith. There is no biblically prescribed timetable for a person's conversion. Neither did the apostles set evangelistic quotas for individual churches. The seed of faith in each unique human being should be allowed to grow according to its God-appointed schedule (Mark 4:26-28).

*Fear Appeals.* A cartoon shows a mother and child sitting at dinner while a thunderstorm rages outside. The mother says, "Thunder and lightning are God's way of saying, 'How come you didn't eat your lima beans?' " We all need an emotional push at times to help us move into action and do what we know we should do. But we must have a clear understanding of what we are doing, and why. An old revival technique is to arouse high anxiety with a vivid message of hell and its torment, tell the listener he can alleviate that anxiety by walking down the aisle, then coax him further with an emotion-charged invitation song. (There is no precedent in scripture for this kind of persuasive technique.) The wrath of God is an important biblical doctrine (See John 3:36, Rom. 5:9, Heb. 10:26-31). Our reverent fear of God motivates us to persuade men (2 Cor. 5:11). But the New Testament picture of discipleship is one of persons committing to a lifelong walk with a living Lord in response to his gracious love. An impulsive or uninformed decision made in a moment of emotional vulnerability, or a commitment based solely on fear, will not provide a firm foundation for a lifetime of faith.

## Paul's Superior Models of Evangelism

In contrast to defective approaches to evangelism that he saw, Paul offered the Corinthians some superior models for Christian torchbearers:

*The Presence: the Aroma of Christ* (2 Cor. 2:14-16). You can still walk upon the stones of the Via Sacra in the Roman Forum, where the armies of Rome marched in magnificent victory processionals. Part of the spectacle of victory was the *smell* of victory, as the priests' fragrant incense spread throughout the city. A Christian torchbearer has a "sweet smell" to his life; you might say he is a breath of fresh air to those around him. His very presence is hopeful, joyous, victorious. The quality of his life will "make the teaching about God our Savior attractive" (Tit. 2:10) to others. As Theresa of Calcutta has said, "Joy is a net of love by which you catch souls."

Picture Mary extravagantly showing her love for Jesus by anointing his feet with expensive nard. John says, "the house was filled with the fragrance of the perfume" (John 12:3). Evangelism begins with the credible, sweet-smelling life whose presence "spreads everywhere the fragrance of the knowledge of him."

*The Proclaimers: the Jars of Clay* (2 Cor. 4:7). I treasure the pieces of ancient Israelite pottery that reside in our living room cabinet, but they are admittedly rather plain and unattractive. Paul paints a dramatic contrast: a divine "treasure" (the Christian gospel) entrusted to the safekeeping of a common earthen jar (the Christian proclaimer).

The best proclaimers are invariably those who recognize their own "earthen-ness"—their weaknesses and limitations. God calls us to be useful vessels, not ornamental vases. So when we proclaim his news, we must not pretend to be what we are not; the greatest impression we make for God may well be to show others what his power can do with an old clay pot like ourselves!

In *The Fight* John White invites us to think of a signpost by the road, telling people how to get to where they want to go. What matters is not the beauty of the signpost, but whether its lettering is clear and it points in the right direction. If the signpost calls too much attention to itself, the traveller may miss the essential information. Again, the Christian proclaimer does not proclaim self, but points to Jesus (2 Cor. 4:5).

*The Persuaders: Christ's Ambassadors* (2 Cor. 5:20). As I write this, representatives of our government and the Soviet Union are arranging a summit meeting, the stated aim of which is to work towards nuclear arms control and world peace. Peace is also the aim of the Christian persuader—to see God's peace come to the lives of men and women. It is not to manipulate or force that decision from people, for we are heralds, not hucksters; ambassadors, not advertisers. Our privileged task is to be faithful spokesmen of the kingdom, calling persons to the peace that comes only when they are reconciled to God. As such, we do not claim "credit" for someone else's faith ("I converted her"), but give the deserved glory to the one whose representatives we are.

The *persuasion* that results in a devoted commitment to Jesus as Lord should be the result of a clear, biblical *proclamation* of Jesus and his kingdom. And so often the door of someone's heart will be opened to the message by the *presence* of a Christian disciple whose life has "the aroma of Christ." So the sequence of the torchbearer's influence is: Presence—Proclamation—Persuasion.

## A Torchbearer's Technique?

Try as we may, we will not find in scripture a specific "technique" used by Jesus in pointing people to God. In fact, he was quite unpredictable! Sometimes he directly called people to costly discipleship; other times he simply served them and left. One day he might give a crystal-clear sermon; the next he might tell a parable not even his closest followers understood. He was a wonderful communicator. But we dare not try to "package his technique," because his technique was nothing less than his holy, genuine servant-life. The Father is more concerned that we be conformed to his likeness (2 Cor. 3:18) than that we attempt to mimic his methodology.

Not surprisingly, it is when we relate to outsiders as the Lord did, that we find them most responsive to his gospel. Dr. Flavil Yeakley interviewed hundreds of individuals who had been approached by Christians sharing their faith; some had converted to Christianity and remained faithful, some had converted and dropped out, and some had not converted. He asked these people how they perceived the Christian who was attempting to evangelize them: as "a teacher teaching a lesson," as "a salesman selling a product," or as "a friend discussing a matter of mutual interest." What he discovered was striking and instructive. Seventy-one percent of the converts who remained faithful perceived the Christian was a *friend.* By contrast, 85% of the dropouts were "evangelized" by someone they perceived as a "salesman," and 87% of those who did not convert saw the person as a "teacher."[2]

A person merely transmitting religious information did not seem to have much impact. Someone who manipulated with sales techniques could elicit a conversion of sorts, but not a lasting commitment. But the torchbearer who cared, who genuinely befriended the searching person, and who shared a faith he could sincerely witness to, made all the difference. "We loved you so much that we were delighted to share with you not only the gospel of God but our lives as well" (1 Thess. 2:8). This is the Jesus-style of torchbearing.

## Developing Your Own Style of Torchbearing

In sharing our faith, as much as in any other form of communication, we must speak from the heart—honestly, clearly, and sincerely. The most effective witness is the one who finds a style of torchbearing that makes best use of his gifts and personality, that allows him to be natural and comfortable, not uptight or affected. Some suggestions:

• Pray for "open doors" into people's lives—opportunities to love, to care, to share the good news (Col. 4:3, 1 Cor. 16:9).

• Serve people, with no hidden agendas. Jesus served many who became disciples but also served many who did not, simply because it was right to serve others (Luke 17:12-19).

• Prepare for verbal torchbearing (1 Pet. 3:15). Have some alternatives in mind, such as: "How about reading through Luke

with me?" or "Here's a tape I'd like to hear your thoughts on."
But also . . .

• Don't force a preset technique or curriculum on people.
Listen carefully to discover their personal needs and questions.

• Talk about Jesus. Help people see his vitality, his human-
ity—how real he is to you. Most people have a very incomplete
or distorted view of the Master.

• Ask good questions. Gently probe: "Have you actually
read the Bible?" "Where did you come by that idea?" "Do you
realize that Jesus had many of the same frustrations with religion
that you have?"

• When someone asks you a tough question, don't be afraid
to say, "I don't know . . . but I'd like to study it and get back
with you." You don't have all the answers—so admit it.

• Avoid religious jargon. Non-Christians are often confused or turned off by "church-talk" ("save souls," "take up a
cross," "born again"). Express the good news in plain language,
in your words.

• Finally, relax. Sow the seed of the Word personally,
genuinely, faithfully. Then leave to God, the Lord of the harvest,
the incredible work of making faith grow in human hearts
(1 Cor. 3:5-9).

[1] John R. W. Stott, "The Messenger and God," *Believing and Obeying Jesus Christ,* John W. Alexander, ed. (Downers Grove, Ill.: IVP, 1980), pp. 30-43.
[2] Flavil R. Yeakley, Jr., *Why Churches Grow* (St. Louis: Anderson's, 1977), p. 59.

# 13

## *How Shall I Talk to God?*

A few years ago during a college football game in Florida, a plane flew over the stadium pulling a banner which read, "Linda, will you marry me? Love, Rodney." In the crowd below an excited Linda turned to Rodney and exclaimed, "Yes!" But a rattled Rodney responded, "No!" The aerial proposal had been arranged by another Rodney for the benefit of another Linda! Right message, wrong receiver.

When we speak from our hearts, we want to make sure that the right message gets through clearly to the right receiver. We are concluding our biblical study of communication with a chapter on prayer. For of all the communicating we do, speaking with God may well be the most important. But often it is here that we struggle most to get our messages through to the right receiver. Here we sometimes feel most inept, most tongue-tied. We wonder, in the words of a great old hymn, "What language shall I borrow, to thank Thee, dearest Friend?"

How shall I talk to God? Surely my thoughts are too foolish, my words too inadequate, my lips too unclean. There is something terribly presumptuous about prayer, about finite and flawed humans attempting to speak to an infinite and perfect God.

165

Abraham sensed it: "I have been so bold as to speak to the Lord, though I am nothing but dust and ashes" (Gen. 18:27).

And yet, amazingly, we find ourselves in scripture beckoned at God's own invitation to approach the throne of grace confidently (Heb. 4:16), to draw near to him (Heb. 10:22). Not only may we invite God to intervene in our lives, he even invites us to have a small voice in the outworking of his eternal purposes in history. He turns a listening, loving ear to our petitions, and promises to act on them in accord with his perfect will (1 John 5:14).

### Right Language or Right Heart?

When we are addressing royalty, government leaders, or judiciary members, etiquette dictates that we get the forms of address right: "Your highness," "your excellency," "your honor." But how should we address the one most worthy of honor and respect? The Bible gives us surprisingly few instructions. In the Old Testament we find the Israelites taking great care not to call him by name at all. They made "Yahweh" (or Jehovah) unpronounceable by shortening it to the vowel-less YHWH. When the name of God appears in a text to be read aloud, the Jewish reader—still today—orally substitutes "Adonai" (the Lord) in its place.

Just as Jesus was not preoccupied with religious titles (Matt. 23:7-10), so God seems less interested in the words of the worshiping person than in his or her *heart:*

> "Who may ascend the hill of the Lord?
> Who may stand in his holy place?
> He who has clean hands and a pure heart."
> (Ps. 24:3-4)

Again the heart must be acknowledged as the primary organ of communication. Any worship that is mere "lip-service" is vain worship, non-worship. Quoting Isaiah, Jesus indicts the smooth, facile ways and words of many religious leaders: "These people honor me with their lips, but their hearts are far from me. They worship me in vain . . . " (Mark 7:6).

The fundamental issue of prayer lies not in form or mechanics: vocal or silent, kneeling or standing, eyes closed or open, hands folded or uplifted. The issue is, are we making contact with God at the heart level? The Father looks deep into our hearts to know us as we truly are (1 Sam. 16:7, Acts 1:24). What do our hearts say?

Prayer is so much more than finding the "right" words, because prayer can go so far beyond where words alone can take us—into our most profound and inexpressible needs, fears, hopes, and joys. Prayer, like all real communication, is an inside-out process. The actual language of prayer becomes an important concern only as it reflects the inner man or woman. Additionally, the wording of prayers has special importance when God's people come together to address the Father publicly and corporately with words of praise and petition.

## When We Pray Together

As I was growing up, the midweek church service was called the "prayer meeting." That phrase well describes many of the assemblies of the first Christian community. In Acts, Luke pictures them in regular prayer together: before Pentecost (1:14); just after Pentecost (2:42); as opposition begins (4:24,31); during Peter's imprisonment (12:12); when they part company (21:5). Corporate prayer was clearly one of the primary spiritual bonding experiences for this brand-new church of Jesus Christ.

In his book *Prayer*, George Buttrick raises the question, "Can't a man pray without belonging to a church?" and responds, "The only answer is, "Yes and No.' If we must choose one word or be shot at sunrise, the answer then is, 'No.' "[1] He was not suggesting that prayer is the right of church members only, but was making the point that Christian fellowship is vitally and essentially important to one's prayer life. Prayer is not intended to be exclusively an individual experience. A musician who

always plays his instrument solo is greatly impoverished for
never having been part of a symphony.

## Leading Public Prayer

When Sally in the *Peanuts* strip was called on in Sunday
School to lead her class in prayer, she adapted the only prayer
she knew: "Now I lay us down to sleep . . . " The differences in
private and public prayer are much greater than simply changing
from first person singular to first person plural.

When someone stands to lead the congregation in prayer,
he shoulders a responsibility which calls for serious forethought.
His task is to express the shared faith of the church family:
"Before our Father's throne, we pour our ardent prayers; our
fears, our hopes, our aims are one, our comforts and our cares."
For that moment he must subordinate his private concerns in an
effort to articulate what he has carefully considered to be the
broader prayer needs of the assembled body. If we use the
prayer-songs of the Psalms and the prayers of Jesus as models
for corporate prayer, then a public prayer should convey a strong
emphasis on praise, thanksgiving, and trust.

Once a particularly impressive public prayer was described
in print as "the finest prayer ever offered to a Boston audience."
For the prayer leader, there will always be the temptation to
"sound good," to offer the prayer to the audience rather than to
God. Jesus etched in our minds unforgettable pictures of street-
corner prayermakers (Matt. 6:5 and Luke 18:10-12). Those of us
who lead in congregational prayer must be more concerned with
our brothers' and sisters' needs than with their applause.

The leader must be especially careful not to be guilty of
what Jesus in Matthew 6:7 calls "vain repetitions" (KJV) or
"heaping up empty phrases" (RSV). Meaningful words can lose
their power to communicate when used over and over again as
liturgical formulas. Consider this Lord's Supper prayer: "Father,
we thank you for this fruit of the vine which to us as Christians
represents the shed blood of our Lord and Savior Jesus Christ on

the cross of Calvary. May those of us who partake do so in a worthy manner. In Jesus' name. Amen."

Such might be a fine prayer for someone just beginning to lead publicly. But experience and maturity should teach a leader to use a wider variety of words and phrases when he focuses afresh the minds of the congregation on the Supper. The late Batsell Barrett Baxter cautioned prayer leaders against "turning off the mind" without "turning off the tongue" (*Speaking for the Master*).

## Learning to Pray from Jesus

But what about my personal prayer life and language? Let's go to the gospels and ask, "Lord, teach us to pray" (Luke 11:1). There are seventeen different references in the gospels to Jesus' practice of prayer, plus many other implied references. Our Lord gave careful attention to his prayer life, doing whatever was necessary to assure enough time and privacy for his talks with the Father (Mark 1:35).

The wording of several of his prayers has been preserved for us: the model prayer (Matt. 6:9-13); the thanksgiving prayer (Luke 10:21-22); the prayer at Lazarus' tomb (John 11:41-42); the intercessory, or high-priestly prayer (John 17); the Gethsemane prayers (Matt. 26:39-44); and the prayers on the cross (Matt. 27:46, Luke 23:34,46).

What can we learn from the prayer language of Jesus? We immediately notice his repeated use of the very personal word "Father" in addressing God. We find him articulating a range of feelings: joy, anguish, thanksgiving, forsakenness. His was a simple eloquence—not flowery, but direct and to the point ("let this cup pass"). He addressed specific needs, such as (in the model prayer) obedience, daily provision, forgiveness, and deliverance. His wording and manner were for the most part what we would expect in a normal conversation (see John 17).

Of all the characteristics we can point to in Jesus' manner of prayer, one of the most striking is the *variety* of "styles" that he used. He prayed in public, he prayed in private. Sometimes his prayers were brief and spontaneous, sometimes lengthy and well-ordered. Sometimes he was quite succinct, as in the model prayer (which was probably intended more as a suggested outline to be followed than a formula to be recited); sometimes he was repetitive, as in the thrice-repeated Gethsemane prayer. Prayer was not a stiff religious exercise for Jesus of Nazareth. It was as vibrant and multi-dimensional as the rest of his life in God.

What can we learn from Jesus? Not so much a glossary of prayer words, but the model of a relationship within which prayer is natural and appropriate in every life setting. Again, let us fix our eyes on Jesus. Using him as our prayer model, Elton Trueblood counsels, "the procedure is to soak ourselves in the model and then to pray freely."

### Great Words of Prayer: "Father"

As we attempt to put our thoughts and feelings into words of prayer, certain key biblical terms come into regular use. Let's look again at some vital words that often suffer from the curse of familiarity.

Jesus taught us in his model prayer to call upon God as "our Father" (Matt. 6:9). The remarkable word he used was the Aramaic *abba*, preserved for us in Mark's gospel as Jesus prays in the garden, "Abba, Father" (Mark 14:36). Paul likewise calls attention to this special term by retaining the original in Romans 8:15 and Galatians 4:6.

To address God as "Abba" in first-century Jewish society was bold, audacious, and absolutely unprecedented. Writes Joachim Jeremias, "Nowhere in the literature of the prayers of ancient Judaism . . . is this invocation of God as *Abba* to be found." For "Abba" was a child's word, a babbling sound. "Abba" and "Imma" in ancient Aramaic correspond linguistically to "Dada" and "Mama" in modern English.

To the religious establishment of Jesus' day, "Abba" was no doubt shockingly irreverent in the familiarity with God it presumed. They did not grasp that part of the reason the Messiah

**66**

*Out of the
overflow of the heart the
mouth speaks*

**99**

came was that man might dare to "draw near" to God. In token and expression of this amazing nearness, Jesus authorized for our use this simple, intimate form of address. What a transforming realization to know that in our prayers today, and when we stand before him face to face, we may in Christ call Almighty God, "Abba, Father."

### "In Jesus' name"

The early Christian called it simply, "the Name" (Acts 5:41). Paul described it as "the name that is above every name" (Phil: 2:9). The Name is *Jesus,* chosen specifically by God for his son. It was an ordinary name—*Yeshua* in Hebrew, *Iesous* in Greek—with an extraordinary meaning: "God saves."

What do we communicate to ourselves and others when we make our prayers "in Jesus' name"? Several things: First, that prayer is a privilege made possible by Jesus, our mediator with the Father (1 Tim. 2:5) and our "living way" to him (Heb. 10:20). Second, that we come before God as those who *belong* to Jesus: having been baptized in his name (Acts 2:38), we now have spiritual life in his name (John 20:31), and we do all in his name (Col. 3:17). And third, that Jesus has authorized us to make our prayer requests to God (John 14:13-15, 15:7).

Using the Name is a profound privilege; we dare not use it casually or selfishly. Recall the painful lesson learned by the "name-dropping" sons of Sceva, seven would-be exorcists who tried to invoke the name of the Lord Jesus to cast out evil spirits. They wanted the power that went with the Name, but they wanted it apart from the commitment signified by its wearing. "Jesus I know and Paul I know about, but who are you?" cried the malevolent spirit as it sent them scurrying away naked and bleeding (Acts 19:15-16).

There is no specific biblical command or example requiring us to verbalize "in Jesus' name" with every prayer. The phrase does not appear in Scripture as some liturgical formula. So let us not recite it as compulsory ritual but use it as a wonderful, regular reminder of how it is that we come before God: because of Jesus, in union with Jesus, enabled by Jesus.

## "Amen"

What does "amen" mean? I have a sneaking suspicion that Gabriel, our two year-old, thinks "amen" means "Let's eat!" For too many of us, "amen" is simply prayer's verbal period, signifying "The End." But the term has a specific meaning, stating that we have listened to, understood, and affirmed the prayer—otherwise, Paul says, we cannot honestly say our "Amen" (1 Cor. 14:16). Describing congregational worship in the mid-second century in his *Apology*, Justin Martyr says of the one presiding over communion: "When he completes the prayers and thanksgiving, all the people sing out their assent by saying, 'Amen.' 'Amen' in Hebrew means 'May it be so.' "

This ancient word can be traced back to early Israelite worship (1 Chron. 16:36), and was used to affirm not only prayers but oaths, blessings, and curses. Within our prayers today it has two primary meanings: *affirmation*—"Yes, this is true, this I believe" (see Eph. 3:21, Rev. 5:14); and *petition*—"Let this be so, according to your will" (Rev. 22:20).

"Amen" is both a thrilling and sobering response, for it identifies what is real and true. Jesus liked to introduce his sayings with *"Amen* I say to you" (Matt. 5:18, 26; 6:2—translated "Truly" or "I tell you the truth"). From ancient days God's people have used it to signal not only their belief, but their readiness to accept the consequences of that belief. Thus an old preacher used to prod his listeners by asking, after he had read from the word, "Do I hear an 'Amen'?"

## Honest to God

Kermit the Frog sings a wistful song as he wrestles with who he is: "It's not that easy being green, . . . It seems you blend in with so many ordinary things." We may at times sing a similar song. It's not that easy being a human being, being ordinary, being the person we want to be before God. Life as a Christian disciple is a continual struggle to conform our wills to the Father's will. And the avenue by which we bring the human struggle to the Father is prayer.

When the prophet Jeremiah was about 40, he went through a kind of spiritual mid-life crisis that resulted in some of the rawest, bluntest prayer language recorded in scripture. He cries out to God:

"I would speak with you about your justice: Why does the way of the wicked prosper?" (12:1).

"I sat alone because your hand was on me. . . . Will you be to me like a deceptive brook, like a spring that fails?" (15:17-18).

"O Lord, you deceived me, and I was deceived; you over-powered me and prevailed" (20:7).

Sometimes Jeremiah's complaints went too far, and God rebuked him and called him to repentance (15:19-21). But what is admirable about the prophet's prayers is their total honesty and transparency. When Jeremiah experienced struggle, or pain, or rejection, or even unbelief, he took it to God. He agonized in prayer through his "dark nights of the soul," but never backed off from his mission nor gave up his faith.

How "honest to God" are we in our prayers? Do we take the real struggles and questions to him? Do we "wrestle in prayer" like Epaphras (Col. 4:12)? From what we read in scripture, it certainly would seem that effective prayer often requires considerable effort—asking, seeking, knocking, even though at times we may feel like we are, in Buttrick's words, knocking "with bleeding knuckles in the dark."

For the supreme example of honest prayer in struggle with God's will, we go to Gethsemane: " 'Abba Father,' he said, 'everything is possible for you. Take this cup from me. Yet not what I will, but what you will' " (Mark 14:36).

"Thy will be done" can be, and often is, just another prayer cliché. But in Jesus' prayer it meant, "Father, I have set before you everything I think and feel and want in this matter. Now let us do what you know to be best, for I trust you to the death."

Jacob wrestled all night with an angelic figure, and for his efforts received a limp and a new name: *Israel*. That great name means, "he struggles with God." For Jesus, for Jeremiah, for Epaphras and many other men and women of faith in God's Word, prayer was the means by which they brought their primary struggles to the Father. And their faith grew, because of— not in spite of—the fact that they were honest to God.

## When Words Don't Come

Daniel Boorstin in *The Discoverers* tells the story of Cape Bojador on the western coast of Africa, past which no ship would sail in the fifteenth century. Terrible rumors circulated about what lay beyond it, so no one passed it for many years. It was, Boorstin says, simply "a barrier in the mind."

Sometimes in our prayer lives we reach an impasse, a brick wall, a barrier in the mind, between us and God. All our communication skills seem to fail us. The feelings run too deep. The confusion is too great.

But for such times God has provided a way beyond the barrier. Paul says, "the Spirit helps us in our weakness. We do not know what we ought to pray, but the Spirit himself intercedes for us with groans that words cannot express" (Rom. 8:26). The Holy Spirit that is God's gift to every believer (Acts 2:38) makes meaningful prayer possible even in our times of weakness and silence. The Father still hears "those agonizing longings which never find words" (J. B. Phillips).

What a great reassurance, to know that God's knowledge of our struggles is not limited by our feeble vocabularies! Though our prayers may be wordless, still our sympathetic high priest Jesus brings our weaknesses to a merciful Father (Heb. 4:15-16). Still God searches our hearts through the Spirit he has given us (Rom. 8:27).

> Prayer is the soul's sincere desire, uttered or unex-
> pressed,
> The motion of a hidden fire that trembles in the
> breast.
>
> James Montgomery

## The Language of Relationship

Is there any act of communication more important than prayer? Here we open our hearts to the Father, honestly, boldly, confessionally. Here we learn to articulate—for our benefit, not God's—who we are and whom we seek to become. Here we give expression to the deep loves and longings from which faith grows.

Religion has regrettably redefined prayer for many people as something ceremonial and impersonal. But for Jesus, who taught us to pray, prayer was the language of *relationship:* "Abba, Father." What we say to God—verbally and nonverbally, privately and publicly—should be an expression of the relationship he has invited us to share with him in Christ. Religious language can be terribly impotent and even harmful when disconnected from that relationship, but wonderfully powerful when generated from it.

I love to hear my grandfather pray. Now in his middle eighties, he prays with a rich Christian vocabulary that draws from a lifetime of Bible study. When he addresses God, his words reverberate with the majesty and honor befitting the Almighty, the King of Glory. But what makes his prayers powerful is not his impressive vocabulary or distinctive vocal quality. What strikes me first and deepest is this, that I am overhearing part of an ongoing conversation between two old and dear acquaintances. It is the language of a love relationship that has been maturing for over sixty years.

Out of the overflow of the heart, the mouth speaks. May God break our hearts and recreate them in the image of his son, so that when we speak from the heart, we give him glory and make him glad. "May the words of my mouth and the meditation of my heart be pleasing in your sight, O Lord, my Rock and my Redeemer" (Ps. 19:14).

[1]George Buttrick, *Prayer* (New York: Abingdon Press, 1942), p. 238.
[2]Joachim Jeremias, *The Central Message of the New Testament* (New York: Charles Scribner's Sons, 1965), pp. 19-20.